WEST BROMWICH
MEMORIES
TERRY PRICE

The History Press

First published in 2006 by
Sutton Publishing Limited

Reprinted wih revisions in 2008
Reprinted 2010, 2011, 2017

The History Press
The Mill, Brimscombe Port, Stroud,
Gloucestershire, GL5 2QG
www.thehistorypress.co.uk

Copyright © Terry Price, 2006, 2017

Title page photograph: The Oak House,
c. 1930. Although built sometime between
1490 and 1510, the first documented
occupant, in 1634, was one Thomas Turton.
During the 1890s this house was purchased,
and afterwards restored, by Alderman Reuben
Farley who on 25 July 1898 presented it to the
town for use as a museum. *(T.J.H. Price)*

British Library Cataloguing in Publication Data
A catalogue record for this book is available from the
British Library.

ISBN 978-0-7509-4427-4

Typeset in 10.5/13.5 Photina.
Printed and bound in England.

Dedicated to my wife's parents,
Beatrice & John Morgan Thompson,
the best in-laws in the world

Other books by the author
Great Bridge & District • Great Bridge Memories
Great Bridge Revisited • West Bromwich People & Places

CONTENTS

South Staffordshire tramcar No. 15 operating on the Birmingham–Wednesbury route waits for passengers at Dartmouth Square, *c.* 1910. On the left, behind Reuben Farley's ornamental drinking fountain, are the High Street bakery premises of Joseph Broadhead. Note the advertisement on the side of the tram for J.F.W. Bodenham, ladies' tailor. *(Ken Rock)*

An aerial view of the Dartmouth Square area of West Bromwich town centre showing (centre) the new multi-storey telephone exchange nearing completion. c. 1974. The building was subsequently converted into the Howard Johnson Hotel. and following a further change of ownership it became known as Days Inn. the highest elevation multi-level building in the UK. The name has recently changed to Premier Travel Inn. (*T.J.H. Price*)

INTRODUCTION

West Bromwich has been the birthplace of many famous people who for various reasons have brought great honour to the town. Alderman Reuben Farley (1826–99) looms large for his magnificent contribution to its growth and advancement during the latter half of the nineteenth century and tributes to this great benefactor can still be observed throughout the borough. In the literary field we have had the brothers David Christie Murray (1847–1907) and Henry Murray (1859–1937), both novelists, while Jessie Pennington's sporting achievements at West Bromwich Albion Football Club between 1903 and 1922 are legendary. Television political analyst, MP and journalist Brian Walden was born in the town (Church Vale) as were pop musicians Robert Plant (Lodge Nursing Home) and Phil Lynott (Hallam Hospital). There are, of course, many others who have achieved some degree of fame after being born in West Bromwich but, in terms of world recognition, no-one can compare with the accomplishments of our very own Madeleine Carroll both as a Hollywood actress and as one of the world's great humanitarians. It is difficult for the present-day generation to appreciate just how big a film star she became during the late 1930s and early 1940s when, at the pinnacle of her career, she was the highest-paid actress in Hollywood, earning more than a million dollars in one year alone. Madeleine, surprisingly, was never honoured by Britain or West Bromwich for either her acting success or her outstanding humanitarian work; both during and after the Second World War, however, her contribution to the war effort was recognised by the American and French governments who respectively awarded her the American Medal of Freedom and the Legion of Honour. In the following years she also received many other honours from countries all around the world.

Edith Madeleine Carroll was born at 32 Herbert Street, West Bromwich on 26 February 1906 to parents Hélène and John Carroll. However, my recent examination of the electoral rolls covering this period show that in 1907 the even numbers in Herbert Street from 28 upwards were increased pro rata, with Madeleine's house becoming the present day No. 44. This discovery means therefore that anyone who has visited Herbert Street in the past to photograph the outside of No. 32, without having this knowledge, has taken pictures of the wrong house! Madeleine's father, who in 1902 was a founder member of the West Bromwich Municipal Secondary School teaching staff, came from Kilduff, County Limerick in Ireland while her French born mother, a devout Catholic, was from Paris. Consequently, Madeleine was baptised at St Michael and the Holy Angels Roman Catholic Church, High Street, West Bromwich on 25 March 1906 by Father John Fox. John Carroll's brother Thomas became her godfather. On 31 August the following year Madeleine's sister Marguerite Marie Carroll was born. The address on the birth certificate was recorded as the renumbered 44 Herbert Street. In 1910, aged four, Madeleine enrolled at The Elms, a private school located in Upper High Street, West Bromwich, which was under the ownership of John and Harriet Silvester. Their unmarried daughters Alice, Annie and Margaret were among the teaching staff. Such was Madeleine's progress that on 7 September 1915 she gained entry into the West Bromwich Municipal Secondary School when she was only nine years of age and of course by this time she could also speak fluent French. After passing her matriculation exam and leaving the secondary school on 20 July 1923 she went on to obtain a BA in languages at Birmingham University in 1926. Her aim was to enter the teaching profession like her father but it was while at university that she made her acting debut in a students' production of *Salma*, an experience which was to dramatically change the course of her life. After a brief teaching appointment at a school in Hove, and against her father's wishes, she decided to pursue her acting ambitions and headed for London, where in 1927 she made her professional debut in a West End stage production of *The Lash*. Soon afterwards Madeleine appeared in her first silent film, *The Guns of Loos*, which was shown at the Imperial Cinema, West Bromwich in February 1929. Madeleine went on to make a total of twenty British and twenty-three American films, the most famous of which was Alfred Hitchcock's *The 39 Steps* which was shown on the opening night of the Tower Cinema, West Bromwich on Monday 9 December 1935. Her status as a major star was further enhanced after moving to Hollywood where in 1937 she was also hailed as the most beautiful woman in the world by film director James Montgomery Flagg. In 1943 after completing her fortieth film *My Favourite Blonde* with Bob Hope, Madeleine, now an American citizen, surprised everyone in Hollywood (and her parents) by giving up acting at the peak of her career to work as a Red Cross nursing orderly on the battlefields of war-torn Europe, changing her name in the process to Madeleine Hamilton

to avoid publicity. At the end of the war, after serving in France, Germany and Italy where she came under fire on many occasions, she was honoured by countries around the world. During and after the war Madeleine was also responsible for establishing and financing two orphanages in France for displaced children. In 1946 she became one of the first ambassadors for UNICEF (United Nations International Children's Emergency Fund) and for many years afterwards she toured the world on a fundraising campaign on their behalf. In 1948 she was voted Woman of the Year by the National Conference of Christians and Jews and in 1949 became the first woman to give a keynote speech to Rotary International in New York, again on behalf of UNICEF. Madeleine made only three more films after the Second World War, the last was *The Fan* (1949), and following a few radio and television appearances she finally retired in 1963 to a farm near Paris. On 2 October 1987, aged eighty-one, Madeleine Carroll, one of Britain's unsung heroines, died in San Pedro, Marbella, Spain.

With 2006 being the one hundredth anniversary of Madeleine's birth, it is pleasing to note that Sandwell Council has grasped the opportunity to celebrate her achievements by agreeing to incorporate a suitable memorial into the design of the new West Bromwich Town Square, which is due for completion this year. The citizens of West Bromwich can feel justifiably proud of this remarkable lady whose Black Country upbringing undoubtedly instilled in her a social conscience for the well-being of those less fortunate than herself.

Within the pages of this book is another selection of photographic memories depicting not only moments associated with Madeleine Carroll's life but also local scenes and the many social activities which have taken place over the last 100 years in our once-glorious town of West Bromwich.

Terence J.H. Price
May 2006

Chapter One

Madeleine Carroll

Madeleine Carroll
1906–87
Actress and Humanitarian.
Born 32 Herbert Street, West Bromwich.
Proclaimed by American film director James Montgomery Flagg in 1937 to be the most
beautiful woman in the world.
(T.J.H. Price)

Copies of Madeleine and Marguerite Carroll's birth certificates showing differing Herbert Street property numbers although the sisters were both born in the same house. Only recently has it been discovered that all even numbers above No. 28 were increased pro rata in 1907 following the removal of six suffix letters (see page 9). Consequently this renumbering has resulted in many of Madeleine's devotees taking photographs of the wrong house. (*T.J.H. Price*)

			7		SANDWELL WARD, div. 1, dis. 1.

No.	Names of Voters in full, Surname being first.	Place of Abode.	Nature of Qualification.	Name and situation of Qualifying Property.
209	Adamson William Francis	35 Herbert street	dwelling house	35 Herbert street
210	Fuller Richard	37 Herbert street	dwelling house	37 Herbert street
211	Massey Owen	41 Herbert street	dwelling house	41 Herbert street
212	Aston James	43 Herbert street	dwelling house— successive	39? High street and 43 Herbert street
213	Chatwin John Ambrose	45 Herbert street	dwelling house	45 Herbert street
214	Morris Thomas	47 Herbert street	dwelling house	47 Herbert street
215	Reynolds Henry Charles	2 Herbert street	dwelling house	2 Herbert street
216	Cartwright George	6 Herbert street	dwelling house	6 Herbert street
217	Adams James	8 Herbert street	dwelling house	8 Herbert street
218	Homer Samuel James	10 Herbert street	dwelling house	10 Herbert street
219	Sedgley William Henry	12 Herbert street	dwelling house	12 Herbert street
220	Stokes John	14 Herbert street	dwelling house	14 Herbert street
221	Randle Edward Thomas	18 Herbert street	dwelling house	18 Herbert street
222	Jones Edward Walter	20 Herbert street	dwelling house	20 Herbert street
223	Rushton Arthur	22 Herbert street	dwelling house	22 Herbert street
224	Darby Thomas	24 Herbert street	dwelling house	24 Herbert street
225	Dutton George	26 Herbert street	dwelling house	26 Herbert street
226	Biddlestone William	28a Herbert street	dwelling house	28a Herbert street
227	Wilkes Samuel	28b Herbert street	dwelling house	28b Herbert street
228	Palfreyman William	28c Herbert street	dwelling house	28c Herbert street
229	Morris William	28d Herbert street	dwelling house	28d Herbert street
230	Sykes David	28e Herbert street	dwelling house	28e Herbert street
231	Oliver George, junr.	28f Herbert street	dwelling house	28f Herbert street
232	France John	30 Herbert street	dwelling house	30 Herbert street
233	Evans William	34 Herbert street	dwelling house	34 Herbert street
234	Rudd Charles	36 Herbert street	dwelling house— successive	6 Legge street and 36 Herbert street
235	Oakley Albert Edward	40 Herbert street	dwelling house	40 Herbert street
236	Perry Alfred	42 Herbert street	dwelling house	42 Herbert street
237	Smith George	44 Herbert street	dwelling house	44 Herbert street
238	Gorman William	48 Herbert street	dwelling house	48 Herbert street
239	Brassington Thomas	52 Herbert street	dwelling house	52 Herbert street

Extracts from the electoral rolls of 1905 (above) and 1907 (below) clearly showing the renumbering of houses from No. 28a upwards which had taken place during the latter year. A whole block of residents had their house numbers increased by twelve, from William Biddlestone at No. 28a (top) to Joseph Toy at No. 66 (bottom). John Carroll's house number therefore changed from No. 32 in 1906 to No. 44 in 1907. *(T.J.H. Price)*

			7		SANDWELL WARD, div. 1, dis. 1.

No.	Names of Voters in full, Surname being first.	Place of Abode.	Nature of Qualification.	Name and situation of Qualifying Property.
216	Reynolds Charles Henry	2 Herbert street	dwelling house	2 Herbert street
217	Adams James	8 Herbert street	dwelling house	8 Herbert street
218	Homer Samuel James	10 Herbert street	dwelling house	10 Herbert street
219	Sedgley William Henry	12 Herbert street	dwelling house	12 Herbert street
220	Stokes John	14 Herbert street	dwelling house	14 Herbert street
221	Whitehouse William	16 Herbert street	dwelling house— successive	9 Walsall street and 16 Herbert street
222	Manners John	18 Herbert street	dwelling house	18 Herbert street
223	Jones Edward Walter	20 Herbert street	dwelling house	20 Herbert street
224	Rushton Arthur	22 Herbert street	dwelling house	22 Herbert street
225	Darby Thomas	24 Herbert street	dwelling house	24 Herbert street
226	Dutton George	26 Herbert street	dwelling house	26 Herbert street
227	Bailey William Charles	28 Herbert street	dwelling house— successive	30 Legge street and 28 Herbert street
228	Biddlestone William	30 Herbert street	dwelling house	30 Herbert street
229	Wilkes Samuel	32 Herbert street	dwelling house	32 Herbert street
230	Palfreyman William	34 Herbert street	dwelling house	34 Herbert street
231	Morris William	36 Herbert street	dwelling house	36 Herbert street
232	Sykes David	38 Herbert street	dwelling house	38 Herbert street
233	Oliver George, junr.	40 Herbert street	dwelling house	40 Herbert street
234	France John	42 Herbert street	dwelling house	42 Herbert street
235	Carroll John	44 Herbert street	dwelling house	44 Herbert street
236	Evans William	46 Herbert street	dwelling house	46 Herbert street
237	Rudd Charles	48 Herbert street	dwelling house	48 Herbert street
238	Oakley Albert Edward	52 Herbert street	dwelling house	52 Herbert street
239	Perry Alfred	54 Herbert street	dwelling house	54 Herbert street
240	Smith George	56 Herbert street	dwelling house	56 Herbert street
241	Burns William	58 Herbert street	dwelling house— successive	43 Walter street and 58 Herbert street
242	Gorman William	60 Herbert street	dwelling house	60 Herbert street
243	Carter Ernest Edward	62 Herbert street	dwelling house	62 Herbert street
244	Toy Joseph	66 Herbert street	dwelling house	66 Herbert street

St Michael and the Holy Angels Roman Catholic Church, High Street, West Bromwich pictured in 1911.
On Sunday 25 March 1906 Edith Madeleine Carroll was baptised here by Father John Fox. Madeleine's godparents were her father's brother Thomas O'Carroll (procurator by proxy Richard Egan) and Annette Comteue De Rosière (procurator by proxy Catterina Egan). Thomas O'Carroll eventually became inspector of schools in Ireland. Marguerite Marie Carroll was also baptised at St Michael's by Father John Fox the following year on 5 September 1907. No godfather was registered but her godmother was Edith Tuaillon after whom Madeleine had been given her first name. Hélène Tuaillon, Madeleine and Marguerite's mother, was from the Bercy district of Paris and a niece of Annette Comteue De Rosière, while John Carroll was an Irishman from County Limerick. The original St Michael's church opened in 1832 and was built to a design by Joseph Ireland in an Early English style with a turret at each corner. A large portion of the building cost was financed by the first resident priest George Spencer, the youngest son of the second Earl Spencer, an ancestor of the late Lady Diana Spencer, Princess of Wales. A later priest, John J. Daly, rebuilt the church in 1875–7 on its present site as a memorial to George (Ignatius) Spencer; the spire was added in 1911. *(T.J.H. Price)*

Herbert Street, the birthplace of Madeleine Carroll, as it appeared in 1910. Her house is situated on the extreme left edge of the picture with (up ahead) the Beeches Road entrance to Dartmouth Park. This park would have been a favourite play area for Madeleine and her sister in their early years as toys were forbidden in the house by their father John. *(T.J.H. Price)*

The White Hart at the junction of Walsall Street and Herbert Street, *c.* 1910. The Carrolls' residence is just a few houses away to the right. It is a matter of conjecture whether John Carroll ever availed himself of this hostelry's facilities during licensee Mary Annie Cartwright's tenancy which ran from 1910 to 1938. The pub's name today is the Drunken Duck.
(Bill Inkson)

The Carroll family on a visit to the O'Carroll ancestral home in Kilduff, County Limerick, *c.* 1910. Back row, left to right: Minnie, Annie, Nicholas, the Revd Pat, Maude, Thomas. Middle row: Hélène Carroll (Madeleine's mother), Madeleine's grandparents and Bridget. Front row: Madeleine Carroll, Marguerite Carroll. Curiously only John Carroll is missing although it is possible that he may have been taking this photograph. *(Ciaran O'Carroll)*

Upper High Street showing Thynne Street on the right with Trinity Street opposite, *c.* 1913. The large three-storey building on the left contains the Constitutional Club (No. 62) and The Elms (No. 64), Miss Silvester's private school where Madeleine began her education in 1910. The current 62 High Street, however, incorrectly bears a nameplate saying The Elms whereas the original Elms building (No. 64) is now fronted by a carpet/furniture store. *(Ken Rock)*

In the background of this First World War memorial unveiling ceremony is the original private school building known as The Elms at No. 64 High Street, where Madeleine received her primary education. However, when this picture was taken in 1919 it had become the Victory Club, the school having closed a year earlier. *(Rita Harris)*

The Ryland Memorial School of Art (left) and (right) the West Bromwich Municipal Secondary School (later Grammar), Lodge Road, *c.* 1905, where John 'Pat' Carroll became a founder member of the teaching staff when it opened in 1902. On 7 September 1915, at the age of only nine, Madeleine was admitted to the school and placed in class 2A. After passing her matriculation examination in 1923 she obtained a BA in languages, with honours, at Birmingham University in 1926. *(T.J.H. Price)*

Madeleine was joined at the secondary school by her sister Marguerite on 9 January 1917; she too was only nine years old at the time of her enrolment. Marguerite is pictured fourth from left on the fourth row among her fellow pupils just before leaving on 24 July 1924. She had no ambitions to follow an academic career like Madeleine. *(Gladys Welsh)*

John Carroll and his family moved from Herbert Street in 1912 to 7 Jesson Street, pictured here in about 1925 looking towards Beeches Road. The Carrolls' house, where they remained until 1939, can be seen on the right, the far one of two, with an attic room built into the roof space which was probably occupied by someone in domestic service. *(Sue Handford)*

Birmingham University pictured around the time of Madeleine's enrolment; she had left the secondary school two months earlier on 20 July 1923. It was here that she fell in love with acting after appearing in the title role of the Birmingham University Dramatic Society's production of *Salma* in March 1926. Her leading man was later to become the eminent surgeon Professor Alphonso D'Abreu. *(T.J.H. Price)*

Right: A 1929 *Midland Chronicle* advertisement for Madeleine Carroll's film debut. After graduating from Birmingham University, Madeleine secured a teaching position in a ladies private school at Hove, but left after only a few months to pursue her new ambition to become an actress. Her stage debut was in the 1927 West End production of *The Lash*. In 1928 she was given a screen test by British film director Sinclair Hill which resulted in her being offered the leading role in her first silent film *The Guns of Loos*. *(T.J.H. Price)*

Above: The Imperial Cinema, Spon Lane, where Madeleine's first silent film, *The Guns of Loos*, was shown to audiences in her home town during the week commencing Monday 25 February 1929, the day before her twenty-third birthday. The photograph dates from about 1974, shortly before the cinema was demolished to make way for the West Bromwich Ringway. *(Edwin Yates)*

Right: Another advertisement from the *Midland Chronicle* for Madeleine's second silent film which was screened at the Plaza Cinema, Paradise Street for three days only from Thursday 25 July 1929. Note that the cinema appears to close between the two evening performances with no Sunday showings at all. *(T.J.H. Price)*

Left: Madeleine Carroll pictured on the occasion of her marriage to Captain Philip Astley on 26 March 1931. Afterwards she was presented at court to HM King George V. Captain Astley was a personal friend of the Duke of Windsor, the future King Edward VIII of abdication fame. For a while afterwards she contemplated retiring but returned to the silver screen in 1933 with two films, *Sleeping Car* opposite Ivor Novello and *I Was a Spy* with Conrad Veidt. *(Derek Chamberlain)*

Above: An early 1930s portrait of Madeleine for a theatre production of *The Pickwick Papers*. In the beginning Madeleine continued to appear on the West End stage as well as advancing her film career. Her teenage elocution lessons paid dividends when talkies came along, with many fellow actors proving unpopular with cinema audiences once they heard their voices. Madeleine, however, went from strength to strength. Interestingly one of her silent films, *The Crooked Billet*, was held back by the studio for a year before being released with a very skilfully added soundtrack. *(Ruth Cherrington)*

The film that made Madeleine Carroll an international star was Alfred Hitchcock's *The 39 Steps*, made in 1935 and co-starring Robert Donat. The film premiered in June 1935 at the New Gallery Theatre, London, with the Tower Cinema, West Bromwich choosing it later the same year for their opening night on Monday 9 December. This picture of the Tower Cinema was taken on that very day. *(T.J.H. Price)*

Hélène and John Carroll pictured prior to their move from Jesson Street, West Bromwich to 11 Hollydale Drive, Bromley, Kent in 1939. John retired from the Municipal Secondary School in July 1937 after thirty-five years in charge of modern language teaching. In his final year he was also acting Headmaster for several months following the sudden departure of Dr Vernon Lloyd. *(Michael Holloway)*

The Prisoner of Zenda made in 1937 saw Madeleine in a starring role as Princess Flavia playing opposite Ronald Colman. The film, based on an adventure novel by Anthony Hope first published in 1894, was a huge box-office hit and a contributing factor in Madeleine becoming the highest-paid actress in Hollywood. Among the supporting actors in the film were David Niven and Douglas Fairbanks Jnr. This success followed on from lead roles in two films directed by Alfred Hitchcock, *Secret Agent* (1936) and the celebrated 1935 film *The 39 Steps* in which she starred opposite Robert Donat. Her appearance in this movie classic also ensured her place in cinema history as the first in a long line of famous Hitchcock blonde heroines. *The 39 Steps* was remade in 1959 featuring Kenneth More and Taina Elg followed by yet another version starring Robert Powell and Karen Dotrice in 1978. Neither of these two latter films managed to surpass the brilliance of the original. *(T.J.H. Price)*

Madeleine made two films with Gary Cooper, *Northwest Mounted Police* (1940), which was her first colour movie, and *The General Died at Dawn* (1936), the latter being nominated for three Academy Awards. The film was regarded by many as Madeleine's finest acting performance. In 1938 a spoof version was made called *The Major Lied till Dawn*. Madeleine also received great critical acclaim in Hollywood following her appearance in the 1940 film *My Son, My Son*, starring opposite Birmingham-born actor Brian Aherne. The storyline in this moving drama of a wastrel son played by Louis Hayward proved to cinema audiences that given the right material, she was more than just a pretty face. *(T.J.H. Price)*

Tyrone Power and Madeleine Carroll in a scene from their 1936 movie *Lloyds of London* loosely based on the growth of Lloyds Insurance business following the Battle of Trafalgar. Tyrone Power plays the part of Jonathan Blake, a member of the Lloyds Syndicate, while Madeleine is Lady Elizabeth, wife of a venomously rude posturer played by George Sanders. *(T.J.H. Price)*

My Favourite Blonde with Bob Hope was made in 1942, the same year that Madeleine married her second husband, fellow actor Sterling Hayden. Following completion of this film, Madeleine, now an American citizen, gave up acting and volunteered to work for the Red Cross in war-torn Europe. In 1946 she returned to star her forty-first film, *White Cradle Inn* with the then almost unknown Michael Rennie. After her last film (*The Fan*, 1949), Madeleine could claim to have been one of the few actresses in the motion picture industry who had the starring role in every one of her movies. *(Ruth Cherrington)*

Left: Marguerite Carroll pictured aged thirty-three just before she was killed at her Kensington home in the London Blitz of 7/8 October 1940. Madeleine was so devastated by her sister's death that she eventually gave up acting at the peak of her career to work overseas for the Red Cross. *(Derek Chamberlain)*

KILLED IN AIR RAID

Tragic Death of Miss M. M. Carroll

The many West Bromwich friends of the family will regret to hear of the death of Miss Marguerite Mary (" Guiguite ") Carroll, daughter of Mr. John Carroll, former senior French master at West Bromwich Grammar School, and sister of Miss Madeleine Carroll, the film actress. She was killed, with a woman Czech refugee, when their home in London was bombed during a recent air raid.

Miss Carroll was 32 years of age, and was well known in West Bromwich, as are other members of the family.

Mr. Carroll rendered valuable service as French master at the Grammar School, where both his daughters received some of their education, for a period of 35 years. He retired in 1937, and he and his wife then went to live at Bromley, Kent.

Miss Madeleine Carroll, who achieved fame almost overnight when she entered films about 12 years ago, has made many successful pictures, which have always had a special appeal for West Bromwich audiences.

Above: The press announcement of Marguerite Carroll's death which was recorded on the death certificate as 8 October 1940. She was in fact 33 years of age and her second name was Marie. *(T.J.H. Price)*

Left: Madeleine Carroll pictured before receiving France's highest award, the Legion of Honour, from General De Gaulle in January 1946. She also received the Medal of Freedom from the American government, their highest civilian honour, but unfortunately nothing from Britain. As well as converting her French château into an orphanage during the war and financing another afterwards, she became one of the first ambassadors for UNICEF and in 1948 was voted Woman of the Year by the National Conference of Christians and Jews. She retired in 1964 to a farm near Paris after devoting more than twenty years of her life to humanitarian work. Madeleine Carroll died on 2 October 1987 in San Pedro, Marbella, Spain, and sadly her achievements went unrecognised by both Britain and West Bromwich. *(Ciaran O'Carroll)*

Chapter Two

The Town Centre, Lyng & Spon Lane

Carters Green, looking north towards the Farley Clock Tower with Dudley Street (left) and Old Meeting Street (right), *c.* 1938. The four Birmingham corporation tramcars are operating on route numbers 75, Birmingham–Wednesbury; 74, Dudley–Birmingham and the short working 73 between Carters Green and Birmingham. All tramway services in West Bromwich ceased on 1 April 1939.
(National Tramway Museum)

Dartmouth Square at the junctions of Spon Lane (left) and Paradise Street, *c.* 1963. The Bulls Head is on the left with the Dartmouth Hotel opposite, where the landlord was Jack Richard Andrews. Printers Joseph Bates Ltd can also be seen on the corner of Barrows Street on the extreme right. The Dartmouth Hotel, dating from 1834, closed on 9 February 1977 while Peter Copper was the licensee. *(Edwin Yates)*

This picture of Dartmouth Square can be dated fairly accurately as 1912 because it shows the pedestal clock, donated by Cllr J. Archibald Kenrick in that year, in the process of being erected. The clock replaced Reuben Farley's ornamental drinking fountain which, until its removal to Dartmouth Park, had occupied this site since 1885. *(T.J.H. Price)*

Ex-England, Liverpool and Wolves soccer captain Emlyn Hughes switches on the refurbished ornamental drinking fountain in the town centre on 23 October 1989 following its transfer from Dartmouth Park. Emlyn Hughes was at the time a hugely popular panel member on the television quiz game *A Question of Sport*. The fountain, however, has rarely been seen working since. *(T.J.H. Price)*

Patrons of the Minuet Ballroom, Dartmouth Square (above Burton's), line up for a photograph on the first anniversary of the premises opening on 12 January 1953. Back row, second from the left: Gladys Leadbeater. Third row, left to right: Brian Wheatley, Tony Welch, Gilbert Healey, Brian Abel, Tommy Meek, Brian Stone, Brian Knight. Second row: -?-, -?-, -?-, -?-, Mary Harris, Betty Griffiths, Val Moore, -?-, Frances Farmer, Minnie Brough, Pat Pattison. Front row, fifth from left: Robert Robertson, tenth: Fred Chambers. *(Brian Abel)*

The High Street offices and works of spring manufacturers George Salter & Co. as viewed from the top of their north works building opposite, *c.* 1939. Beyond these offices, through the haze, is the Spon Lane area of the town. This world famous firm was established in a small Bilston cottage in 1760, thirty years before moving to West Bromwich. *(Stan Stokes)*

George Salter FC, members of the Birmingham Works League, *c.* 1967. Back row, left to right: Cyril Knowles, Anthony Bailey, Peter Morris, Neil Lewis, Brian Percival, Roger York, Robert Nation, Jimmy Osborne, Ken Brett, Arthur Moore. Front row: John Sheppard, David Fisher, Peter Bartram, Pat Hoban, Robert Priest. *(Roger York)*

The High Street, looking south towards Birmingham Road, *c.* 1930. The tall building on the right, now demolished, contained the offices of George Salter & Co. while opposite the only building immediately recognisable is the Stores public house with its prominent nameplate above the guttering. The property next door, covered with posters, was eventually replaced by a branch of the Midland Bank. *(Ken Rock)*

Ye Olde Wine Shoppe, 89 High Street, *c.* 1950. Licensee Emily Fletcher had managed this pub since 1934, one of the town's longest-serving publicans. Another well-known character connected with this establishment was Jimmy Lee, landlord for a record twenty-four years from 5 October 1961 until 21 February 1985. Having originally been known as The Old Grapes prior to 1882, it was rather appropriate therefore that grapes should turn into wine. *(Andrew Maxam)*

The Central Police Station, corner of High Street and Nicholls Street, decorated for the coronation of King George VI and Queen Elizabeth on 12 May 1937. In the doorway on the left are Superintendent Charles 'Nobby' Clarke and his wife Sarah Ellen while outside the right entrance, from left to right, are Inspector Marchant, Wilfred Louis Smith and Inspector Felton. This building was opened in 1851 and demolished in about 1973. *(Harvey Birch)*

West Bromwich Police Divisional football team, runners up in the Chief Constable's Cup, 1936/37. Back row, left to right: ? Smith, ? Townsend, Frank Woodhouse, William Lawton, ? Evans, ? Brice, ? Haynes, Jack Bentley. Middle row: Inspector Marchant, Jarv Green, Len Podmore, Superintendent Charles 'Nobby' Clarke, Sid Grundy, Bill Adams, Arthur Wright, Inspector Felton. Front row: Harvey Birch, Howard Storry. *(Harvey Birch)*

Second World War Special Constables pictured at the rear of West Bromwich Central Police Station, at the junction of High Street and Nicholls Street, c. 1944. Back row, left to right: -?-, Thomas Howard Homeshaw, -?-, John Ault, -?-. -?-, Pat Payton. Front row, third from left: Superintendent Charles 'Nobby' Clarke. *(Kathleen Homeshaw)*

West Bromwich Auxiliary Women's Police Constables based at the High Street Central Police Station, c. 1945. The jaunty angle of some of these ladies' caps would have raised an eyebrow or two in the disciplined ranks of the police force. Back row, left to right: Jackie Wall, Joyce Boulton, Sheila Wimbury, Doreen Bird, Mary Farrell. Front row: Betty Laycock, Eileen Rowley, Yvonne Garrett, Elsie Smith. *(Betty Bonell)*

Upper High Street, looking towards Dartmouth Square, *c.* 1920. The tall domed building on the corner of George Street (left) belongs to A.J. Turley Ltd, furniture dealers, with Samuel Firkin, pork pie manufacturers, opposite. Harry Kendall at No. 75, picture frame makers, has a very intriguing sign above his shop proclaiming 'wood letters'. The cleared site of these properties on the right now provides vehicular access to Overend Street. *(Ken Rock)*

Elizabeth and Lucy Griffiths' Art Needlework Repository (woolshop), 55 High Street, showing shop assistant Edna Orme standing outside, *c.* 1923. The business was established by Robert Griffiths in 1909 who passed it on to Elizabeth and Lucy in 1918. They continued for another thirty-six years before retiring in about 1954. Many people may also remember John Rex Allen's chemist shop next door on the right at No. 53. *(Frances Davies)*

West Bromwich Albion players pictured on their Halfords Lane training ground apparently practising their defensive strategy for the next match, *c.* 1935! Back row, left to right: Sid Swindon, Jack Sankey, Jack Mahon, Billy Tudor, Norman Male, Lawrie Coen, Billy Light. Front row: Harry Kinsell, Herbert Hunt, Sammy Heaselgrave, W.G. Richardson, Harry Ashley, Jack Screen, Tommy Glidden. *(Herbert Hunt)*

Crowds pictured leaving the Hawthorns in Birmingham Road after the League Division 1 match between West Bromwich Albion and Sunderland on Saturday 25 February 1967. The game resulted in a 2–2 draw. Astle and Fraser were the scorers for the Baggies in front of 22,296 fans. The ground, which is on the corner of Halfords Lane, can just be seen behind the ten pin bowling alley sign. *(Harvey Birch)*

Three Mile Oak, 148 Birmingham Road, *c.* 1982. This hostelry was originally named after an oak tree which stood on the opposite side of the road, near the Dartmouth Cricket Club. One of the pub's more famous landlords was the West Bromwich Albion player and director, Daniel Garbut Nurse, who held the licence from 1910 to 1922. These premises closed in 1990 and were later demolished. *(T.J.H. Price)*

The Vine, 152 Roebuck Street, *c.* 1982. This very popular pub has had comparatively few licensees over the last 150 years – the present landlord Suresh Prabhu Patel has clocked up twenty-eight of them so far. Other long-serving 'gaffers' have included John Lyman (1882–1902), John Turley who served over thirty-five years from 1906 and in more recent times Edith Burford, who was in charge from 2 July 1959 to 19 April 1973. *(T.J.H. Price)*

Beeches Road Methodist Church Sunday School anniversary, *c.* 1965. Back row, left to right: Peter Gadd, Geoff Allport, -?-, David John, Frank Riley, -?-, Alan Hamilton, Eileen Riley, Christine Pritchard, Alan Moore, David Woodcock, Sidney Thorne, Fred Delicott, Tom Rivers. Middle row: Charles Quance, Alice Shorthouse, Edna Quance, Molly Thorne, Doris Gadd, Barbara Riley, Carol Moore, Doreen Parker, Susan Thorne, Barbara ?, Margaret Gregory. Front row: -?-, -?-, ? Maxwell, Roger John, -?-, Susan Garbett, -?-, -?-, -?-, Brian John, -?-, -?-, -?-. *(Carol Reynolds)*

Children's Christmas party at the Warriors Club, Beeches Road, *c.* 1956. The club was operational between 25 September 1945 until about 2000, during which time Alderman Jack Williams successively held the positions of secretary, chairman and president. Those known to be in the picture are, top right: Jack Ryan, top left: Edward Tye, centre left: Edwin Williams, centre right: John Williams, Joyce Williams, Margaret Lovell. *(Jack Williams)*

One of West Bromwich Albion's finest players, Ray Barlow (left), pictured in about 1955 in his tobacconist and confectionery shop at 12 Bull Street which he ran from 1954 until 1963. Also present is another Albion legend, Tommy Glidden (centre), the previous owner from 1934 to 1954, with, on the right, Dennis Dunn who was a vocalist along with Ray's wife Beryl in the Brian Pearsall Band which performed regularly to sell-out audiences at the Adelphi Ballroom. *(Ray Barlow)*

Bull Street, *c.* 1972. Centre right is one of the town's oldest established businesses, Bert Shinton Cycles. Albert Edward Shinton opened his first shop here at No. 17 in 1908 and shortly afterwards also acquired the adjoining property No. 15 (right). By 1926 he had taken over two more shops in Bull Street, No. 1 and No. 3, and then in 1938 also became a radio dealer at 200–2 High Street. *(Charles Smith)*

Furniture dealer Frederick Carless pictured outside his Bull Street shop, *c.* 1910. This business was acquired from Thomas Woodward in 1902 following Frederick's marriage to Thomas's daughter Elizabeth, a dressmaker of 87 Hargate Lane. Between 1936 and 1966 the firm was managed by Ada, Alfred and William Carless who in turn were succeeded by Elsie and Bill Carless. The shop eventually closed in 1984. *(Elsie Carless)*

Thomas Woodward, general broker and house furnisher, 19 (later renumbered 33) Bull Street, *c.* 1900. Thomas ran a similar shop in Dartmouth Street from 1874 to 1878 before moving here in 1886. The premises had been used previously, between 1874 and 1886, by Charles Smith a hay/straw dealer and afterwards by Francis Jones, a dairyman. From left to right: Frederick Carless, -?-, -?-, Elizabeth Carless, -?-, Thomas Woodward. *(Elsie Carless)*

The Overend Stores, off-licence, 123 Overend Street, 7 March 1969, when Shirley Joan Hinson was the licensee. One of the earliest occupants of these premises was John Evans from 1882 until 1894, followed by Mary Lofthouse from 1894 to 1898 and Edith Silvester from 1898 to 1902. The longest serving licensee in more recent times, however, was Elsie Gregory, 8 January 1959 until 12 January 1967. This ex-Darby's off-licence finally closed on 26 October 1970. *(T.J.H. Price)*

Overend Methodist Church pantomime, *Humpty Dumpty*, 1961. Back row, left to right: Bill Udall, Alan Moore, Sid Thorne, John Udall, Geoff Allport, Alan Udall, John Walters, Reg Shaw, Freda Forrest. Middle row: Margaret Hunt, -?-, Fred Delicott, Carol Moore, Doris Stevens, Susan Thorne, Shirley Allport, Doreen Parker, Tony Hallard, Philip Hunt. Front row: -?-, Jill Timmins, Pearl Walters, Marilyn Walters, -?-, -?-, Helena Finney, -?-, -?-. *(Carol Reynolds)*

West Bromwich Spring FC, winners of the Birmingham & District A.F.A. league's A.E. Hills Memorial Shield, 1950/51. Back row, left to right: Bill Shaw, Richard 'Dickie' Parkes, Ron Grigg, Joe McCadden, George Cashmore, Bill Clive, Arthur Hartshorne, Frank Handley, Les Pace. Front row: Ernie Nicholls, Len 'Checker' Perry, Bill Mauldridge, Tom 'Hammer' Haycock, Tom Shadwell, Arthur Norton, Albert Wheatley. *(David Grigg)*

West Bromwich Spring darts and snooker teams, winners of the inter-departmental competitions, *c.* 1956. Back row, left to right: Ivan Birks, Wally Russon, George Cashmore, John Rock, Tony Martin, Tom Haycock. Front row: Ieuan 'Taffy' Davies, Ron Grigg, Les Pace, Bill Clive, Brian Gough. *(Joan Haycock)*

Medley's wireless accessories shop, 89 Spon Lane, *c.* 1930. The business was started by Arthur Medley in a house near Railway Terrace in 1926 where he sold parts for the construction of radios. In 1928 he moved into premises at 89 Spon Lane, next door to Maude Lissimore's shop where he met his future wife Jessie. By 1939 the growth of the business necessitated a move to larger premises further up Spon Lane at No. 25. During the Second World War Arthur Medley taught wireless telegraphy to the Air Training Corps at the YMCA in St Michael Street. It was during this time that he developed an interest in politics and in 1945 he was elected as a Labour Councillor for the Tantany Ward, culminating in him becoming the Mayor of West Bromwich in 1951. A second shop was opened in 1962 at 349 Lower High Street, just twelve months before Arthur died aged sixty-one. The Spon Lane shop closed in 1972 after a compulsory purchase order was issued, but the High Street branch continued with his son Jim Medley at the helm until 1986 when the business finally closed down. *(Jim Medley)*

The Cottage Spring, 42 Spon Lane, situated between Thomas Street and George Street, *c.* 1932. Minnie Withers, the licensee between 1930 and 1934, had previously been the landlady of the Cross Keys in Wood Lane for twenty-two years. After leaving the Cottage Spring she took over the Anchor in the High Street. The Cottage Spring closed during the late 1960s. *(Betty Gibson)*

Right: The Imperial haircutting and shaving saloon, 36 Spon Lane, 1914. Standing on the doorstep is the proprietor Thomas Bernard Taylor who, not long after this photograph was taken, volunteered for service in the First World War during which he unfortunately lost a leg. He was one of only three hairdressers to occupy these premises between the period 1890 to 1950. They were Josiah Tongue 1890–1913, Thomas Bernard Taylor 1913–15 and William Gilbert 1915–50. *(Marjorie Welham)*

Above: Miss May Reynolds' confectionery shop, 197 Spon Lane, *c.* 1936. Before becoming a confectioners in 1890 (owned by Ellen Edwards) it had been a drapery business run by James Skidmore and before him Alfred Harper sold milk from here. In 1934 May Reynolds acquired the business and as a result of her marriage in 1938 the shop's name was changed to Miles. After thirteen years trading the shop closed in 1947. *(Iris Reynolds)*

Right: Usherettes pictured in the foyer of the Imperial Cinema, Spon Lane, *c.* 1957. The film *Keep it Clean*, starring James Hayter, was made in 1956. From left to right: Flo Downing, Margaret Leadbeater, Gladys Wilkes (cashier), Dora Steele, Bert ? (doorman). *(Derek Millward)*

Coronation celebrations for Queen Elizabeth II in Boulton Square, 2 June 1953. Len Harris is pictured with a bandaged wrist and a ladder in his stocking on an Ariel motorcycle while on the slightly leaning elevated rocking horse is South Sea Island girl Rita Harris. In the background on the left are Raymond Rowley and Terry Bunn with, on the right, Philip Orme. What a great example of the joyous atmosphere prevailing all over Britain in those austere times. *(Rita Harris)*

Below: More coronation celebrations in Boulton Square on 2 June 1953. Back row, left to right: Janet Hunter, Dorothy Horton, John Bates, Christopher Wilson. Third row: Pat Tinsley, Michael Maughan Jnr, Irene Ingram, Pauline Freeth, Anthony Smith, -?-. Second row standing: Jean Cadd, Norman Jackson, Doreen Rowley, Phyllis Parkes, Margaret Maughan, Rita Harris, George Dixon, -?-, George Rowley. Front row: Nellie Hill, Daisy Hunter, Kathy Forsyth, Kathy Sheppard, Edith Knight, Norman Bunn, William Bates, Mary Ann Dixon, Mary Fletcher, Amy Bates, Michael Maughan Snr. *(Rita Harris)*

May Day celebrations in Boulton Square, *c.* 1932. Back row, left to right: Rose Holden, Graham Nock, George Green, Minnie Barnfield, -?-, Betty Gordon, Dora Smith. Third row: -?-, Olive Gilbert, Ann Smith, -?-, Hilda Barnfield, ? Barnfield, -?-. Second row: Trevor Abell, Margaret Knight (white hat), Leslie Abell (cap), Clifford Abell (tall lad). Front row: -?-, -?-, -?-, -?-, -?-, Dorothy Abell, Archie Holden, Rita Knight (white hat), Olive Bell. *(Rita Harris)*

Children celebrating the coronation of Queen Elizabeth II in Boulton Square, 2 June 1953. Back row, left to right: Pat Tinsley, Michael Maughan, Irene Ingram, Janet Hunter, Dorothy Horton, John Bates, Pauline Freeth, Christopher Wilson, Anthony Smith, -?-. Middle row: -?-, -?-, -?-, Jean Cadd, Terry Bunn, Ethel Cadd, -?-, -?-, -?-, Irene Horton, -?-, Margaret Fletcher, -?-, Margaret Maughan, Rita Harris, -?-, -?-. Front row: -?-, John Harris, -?-, Leonard Harris, -?-, David Parkes, Brian Tinsley, Christine Reeves, -?-, Pamela Crowshaw, -?-, -?-, -?-, -?-, -?-, -?-, Neil Jenkins, -?-, Alan Crowshaw, Peter Harris. *(Dorothy Pritchard)*

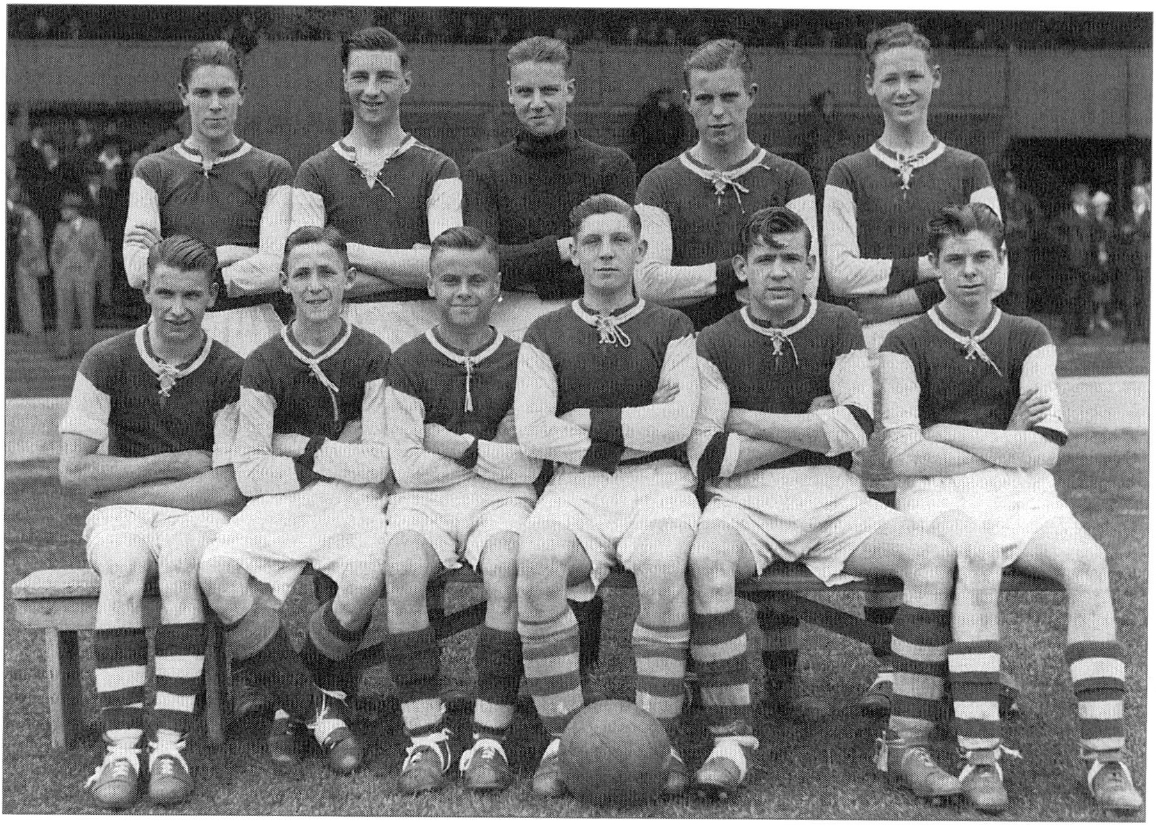

Hawthorn United FC (based in the Spon Lane area), winners of the JOC Intermediate League and Aston Villa Cup, 1939/40. Back row, left to right: 'Algie' Cartwright, Cliff Howell, Harold Jones, Ray Weston, Jack Male. Front row: George Saunders, George Male, Arthur Evans, William Jewkes, Frank Morrall, Eric Westwood. *(Harold Jones)*

The Cricketers Arms, 43 Lower Trinity Street, *c.* 1960. The pub dates from about 1860 when John Woodbridge, who also ran a butcher's business from here, was the licensee. Caleb Hale was the next, from 1874 to 1894, setting a twenty-year tenancy record for these premises. Other landlords were Abraham Jones between 1918 and 1934 and Harry Reynolds between 1936 and 1943. At the time of this photograph Joseph William Haynes was in charge. *(Andrew Maxam)*

The Windsor Castle Inn, 140 Sams Lane, 12 May 1965. Leonard Dee was the landlord at this time. The record for longevity at this pub belongs to the Chapple family who held the licence for thirty years, Robert Henry Chapple was first between 1902 and 1914, then Clara Chapple from 1914 to 1932. These premises closed on 4 October 2001 and Patricia Joan Hughes was the last licensee. The building is currently undergoing a conversion into a restaurant. *(Andrew Maxam)*

Metal Closures FC, winners of the West Bromwich & District Sunday Football League Division 1, the John Colley Cup and the Walsall Conduits Cup, 1957/58. Back row, left to right: Eric Barnes, Jim Bennett, Brian Harvey, Harold Whitehouse, John Humphries, Brian Beckett, -?-, -?-. Front row: Norman Steptoe, Geoffrey Plested, Ted Marsh, Cliff Satterthwaite, Stan Bradbury, Brian Parkinson, -?-, Alan Waterhouse, Ray Bonehill. *(Geoffrey Plested)*

The Wellington Inn, 36 Newhall Street, *c.* 1930. Thomas Arthur Fleet, the pub's longest serving landlord (1913–43), is seen on the doorstep with his wife Eunice and their two children. He was one of only twelve licensees to occupy these premises during its 100-year history, from Aaron Baggot between 1863 and 1874 to Charles Beddoes who was the tenant when it closed in 1963. Edwin Standing, who was also a boot dealer, ran the pub for twelve years between 1874 and 1886 followed by Luther Cotterill between 1886 and 1898 and Elizabeth Robinson between 1898 and 1912. *(Tom Shelton)*

Below: Lyng Lane Social FC, 20 February 1950. Back row, left to right: Joe Bubb, Frank Starkey, Ray Smith, Derek Sorrell, Geoff Wheatley, Maurice 'Nobby' Whitehouse, Sid Hall Snr. Front row: Ronnie Timmins, Horace 'Polly' Payne, Harry Latimer, Stuart Dicken, Sid Hall Jnr. During the early 1950s the team was a force to be reckoned with in the Handsworth League even though they were only successful in three out of six appearances in cup and shield finals: the T.R. Fardell Memorial Cup and Handsworth Cup (both in 1949/50) and West Bromwich Albion Shield (1953/54). In league competitions they were divisional runners-up on four occasions in 1949/50, 1950/51, 1953/54 and 1954/55. *(Eunice Hall)*

A ladies' outing from the Wellington Inn, Newhall Street to Trentham Gardens, *c.* 1958. Back row, left to right: Kate Hanley, -?-. Fourth row: -?-, ? Greenaway, -?-, -?-, Hilda Lloyd, ? Freer. Third row: Mary Bisseker, ? Bisseker, ? Bisseker, Lily Timmins, Rene Hall. Second row: ? Greenaway, Ann Lewis, Floss Davies, Florence Shelton. Front row: -?-, Mary Sperring, Edie Whittingham, ? Whittingham, -?-, Betty Jackson. *(Tom Shelton)*

The Albion Inn, 55–7 Newhall Street, June 1914. In the doorway, first left, is landlord Samuel Southall with Joseph Shelton next to him. Frederick Hill was the longest-serving licensee here, from 1934 to 1955, and when it closed in 1966 James Henry Hope was the last. The posters in the window are advertising the opening night of Kennedy's New Empire Theatre (Plaza/Kings) on Monday 22 June 1914. The pub's frontage was altered in 1920. *(Tom Shelton)*

W.S. Quance, pork butcher, 63 High Street, *c.* 1930. The business was established in 1896 at 67 High Street by William Samuel Quance who four years later transferred the operation to the premises seen in the photograph. Such was his success that in 1910 a second outlet was opened at 305 Rookery Road, Handsworth, followed in 1919 by a third at 86 High Street, West Bromwich, which also had slaughterhouse facilities. During the First World War the firm became the target of anti-German demonstrations after local people with hostile intentions had gathered outside 63 High Street in the mistaken belief that William Quance was of German extraction. The situation was only resolved after a press announcement had threatened legal action against anyone causing civil unrest by challenging the long-standing English ancestry of the Quance family. Following the death of their father in 1948 Frederick William and Charles Henry Quance formed a limited company, W.S. Quance Ltd which, in 1955, included the twins John and Robert Quance. After closure of the Handsworth and 86 High Street branches in 1980, the firm finally ceased trading from their remaining 63 High Street premises in 1984. From left to right: Harry Summers, William Samuel Quance, Charles Henry Quance, George James. *(John Quance)*

The Victoria Inn, 32 Sams Lane (later Lyng Lane), 7 April 1961. At this time Alexander Raeburn Hornby was the licensee having succeeded Harry Reynolds who had been the landlord from 8 February 1951 until 2 July 1959. The record holder, however, was John Raybould, a tenant for twenty-eight years from 1870 to 1898. In the years following M&B's purchase of this inn from Darby's there have been eighteen licensees. *(Andrew Maxam)*

The High Street's central shopping area during the era of 'The Golden Mile' with, in the distance, St Michael's Roman Catholic Church, *c.* 1936. Woolworths can be seen on the left next to Montague Burton, tailors, which had three shops on the High Street. Halford cycles and Zissmans outfitters are on the right with Hudsons Passage in between. *(Jim Houghton)*

High Street looking from Lower Queen Street and the Corner House pub towards Dartmouth Square, *c.* 1962. The whole of this area was pedestrianised during the mid-1970s and is now called Princess Parade. When this highway was constructed in the early nineteenth century town planners decreed that it should not be less than 60ft wide, including the pavements. *(Edwin Yates)*

Paradise Street, looking towards Dartmouth Square, September 1969, where a West Bromwich Corporation Metro-Cammell Weymann-bodied Daimler CVG6 bus is seen waiting outside Johnny's Jewel Box on route No. 220 to Smethwick and Bearwood. In the background, at the rear of this bus, is the Albion Hotel with the old Peacock's store also just visible behind. *(Graham Harper)*

Lower Queen Street, April 1967, where a West Bromwich Corporation Mulliner-bodied Leyland Tiger Cub bus is leaving for Hateley Heath and Great Bridge. Dominating the background is the Kings Cinema which opened as Kennedy's New Empire Theatre on Monday 22 June 1914. After becoming the Plaza Cinema in 1927, a theatre in 1951 and closing in 1957 it quickly reopened as the Kings Cinema. When demolition took place in 1973 a replacement Kings was built, but it too closed in 2002. *(Graham Harper)*

Joseph Bates FC, winners of the Bloxwich Combination Sunday Premier League, the Charity Cup, the Walsall FA Junior Cup and the Horrocks Hobbies Cup, 1974/75. Back row, left to right: Barry Hughes, Alf Clifford, Tyrone Jones, John Garfoot, Edward Whitehouse, Alan Ledbury, Des Shipp, John Morris, Bob Travis, Malcolm Jarvis, Roger York, Albert Williams. Front row: Bob Clews, Stan Maughan, David Hadley, Martin Scott, Brian Hall, Keith Parsons, Martin Hunt. *(Roger York)*

Motor Auctions (West Bromwich) Ltd, Paradise Street, *c.* 1969. The firm was established by Gerry and Dorothy Whitehouse in 1966 within the property which had previously been Peacocks warehouse. Four years later in 1970 the business transferred to Bilport Lane, Holloway Bank, and after a further period of successful expansion was sold to the Arlington Motor Company in 1982. The picture shows cars entering from Barrows Street, with auctioneer Malcolm Mosey, Ron Rowe, Tom and Rene Clay, on the left. Ron Sadler is opposite on the bench. *(Gerry Whitehouse)*

A view of the High Street, with the entrance to Lower Queen Street on the right, 1920. The single-storey building in the centre of the picture and those off to the left were demolished in about 1922 and replaced with a much grander structure, housing such retailers as Woolworths and Montague Burton. It was around this time that the new market hall was constructed with its entrance being incorporated into the new development. *(Ken Rock)*

High Street at the junctions of Lower (left) and Upper (right) Queen streets, *c.* 1914; these are now the respective entrances to the King's Square and Queen's Square shopping centres. The imposing building of greengrocer Joseph Pester is on the left while opposite, behind the lamppost, two of the three balls associated with Phineas & Joseph Samuels' pawnbrokers business are evident. *(T.J.H. Price)*

The interior premises of John Wesley Henn, watchmaker, jeweller, silversmith and optician, 221 High Street, *c.* 1930. The firm was established in 1897 at 3b Bull Street with additional shops opening at 75 Paradise Street (1898) and the property pictured above, in 1910. Henn's Bull Street and Paradise Street outlets closed in 1902 and 1922 respectively, while the High Street shop continued into the 1990s. *(John Quance)*

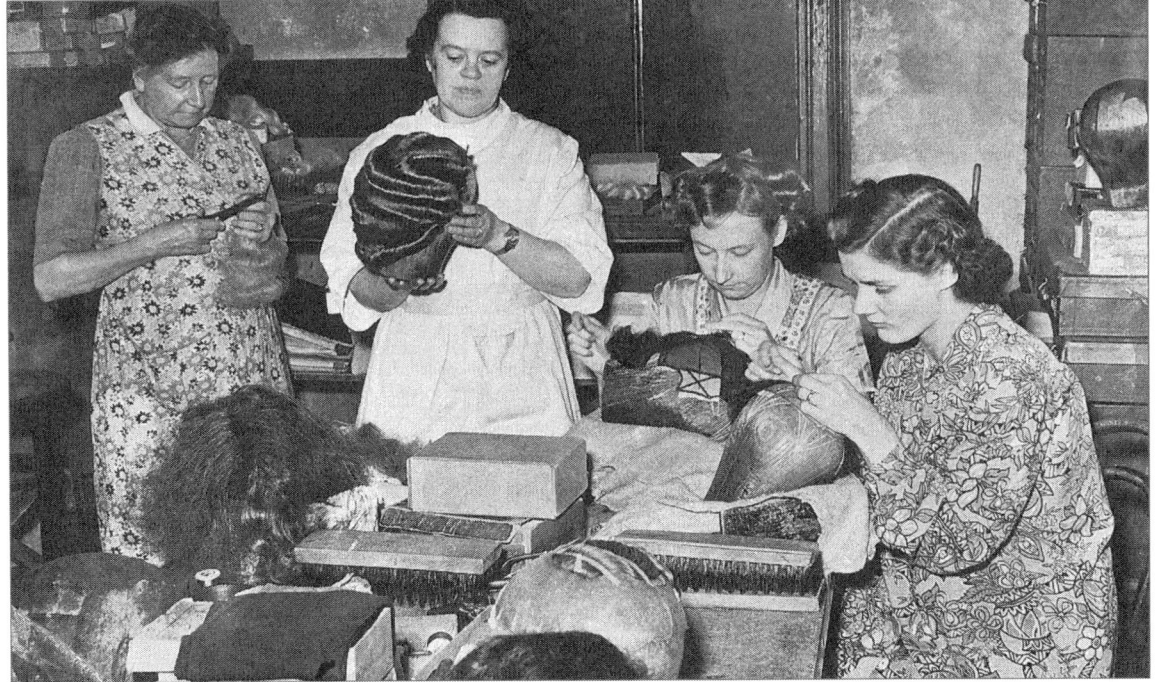

Cammies & Cadman's wig-making department at the rear of the upstairs ladies hairdressing salon, 220 High Street, *c.* 1951. The firm, established in about 1930 by John Harry Cammies, was one of the last in the Midlands to carry on this extremely delicate and skilled work on site. From left to right: Adelaide ?, Louie Lomax, Kathleen Gray, Alison ?. *(Michael Cammies)*

On the left of this High Street picture is the entrance to Upper Queen Street (below the Hovis sign) with Union Passage opposite, beneath the '210' building on the right. This passage became Lower Queen Street in about 1913 when the adjacent buildings were demolished, including the Lion Vaults public house. The Corner House pub, Palace Cinema and Pester's greengrocers became their replacements. *(T.J.H. Price)*

Honved Albion FC, members of the West Bromwich & District Sunday League, *c.* 1957. Back row, left to right: Harry Grainger, Len Winsper, Frank Riley, Micky Morton, -?-, Ron Hughes, Billy Hughes, Eric Plant, -?-. Front row: -?-, Tom Chambers, Desmond Birch, Ron Timmins, Jeff Hickman. *(Alan Hughes)*

The Great Western Hotel, 242 High Street, c. 1982. Until 1972 this pub had the unusual feature of a second frontage in Paradise Street with a connecting entry in between. Joan Florence Nodder, the licensee, served two terms here between 24 July 1969 and 10 January 1980 and again from 22 April 1982 to 5 October 1988. After numerous alterations and changes of ownership it eventually became known as Barnabys. (T.J.H. Price)

The Star & Garter Hotel, 252 High Street, 21 April 1965. This inn has been subjected to a number of 'add on' building works in the years since 1845 when Edward Spittle was the landlord. Leonard John Arnold was the licensee when this picture was taken. The opening with the parked car in it was once known as Star Alley and contained a number of houses. (Andrew Maxam)

High Street, as seen from the open top of a tram passing the junctions of New Street and St Michael Street, c. 1927. William Mason's butcher's shop at No. 273 is on the left, with Alfred Dresden's tailor's premises at No. 254 opposite. This latter property became Harry Playfair's shoe shop in 1938. This part of the High Street is now called Duchess Parade following pedestrianisation which took place in the mid-1970s. (Fred Dyson)

The Electro Mechanical Brake Company (EMB) premises in Moor Street pictured in May 1992 after the removal of its roof. The landlord of the adjoining Leopard public house at the time was Harold Francis Smith. Andrea Berkley was the last licensee before this hostelry was demolished in 1999. *(T.J.H. Price)*

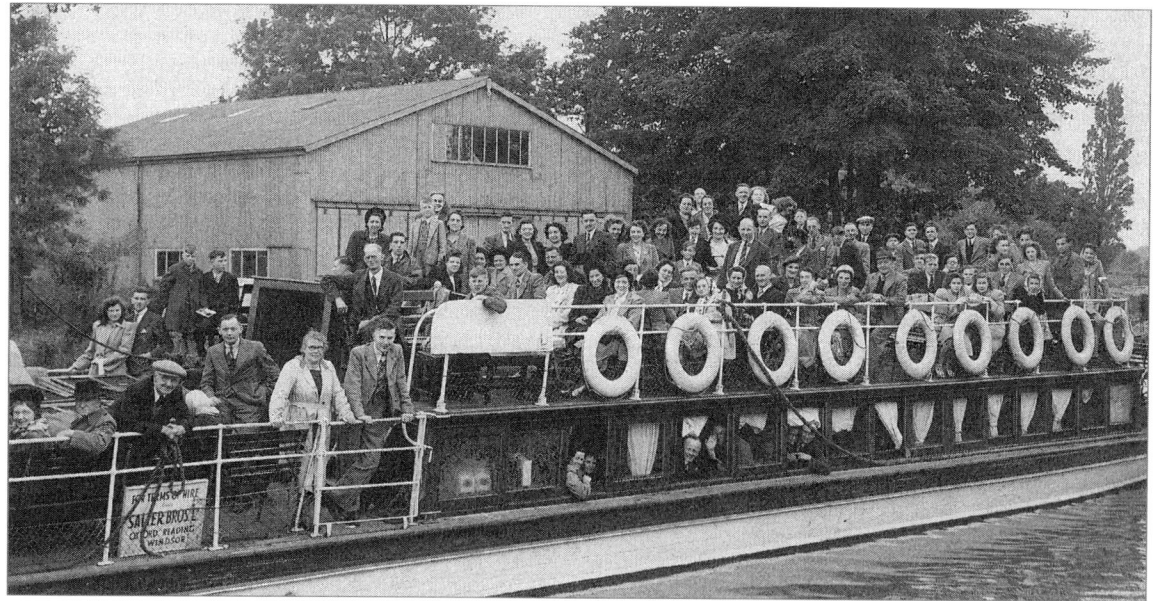

Employees of EMB, Moor Street, on a trip to Windsor along the River Thames, August 1949. Among those on the boat: Fred Simpson, Albert Linney, Derek Ball, Ivy Dyson, Stan Dyson, Ivy Williams, Betty Harrison, Marion Key, Ivy Burns, Pauline Stanton, Geoff Butler, Albert Linney, Eileen Holden, Rita Mills, Fred Mynett, George Law, Dorothy Boyce, Percy Woodman, Malcolm Lee, Jeffrey Stampe, Bernard Walsh, Betty Butler, Margaret Baker, Dennis Woodall, Howard Linney, Kathleen Flanagan, Jean Bayliss, Brenda Deakin, Alan Meredith, Derek Morgan, Frank Whitehouse, Len Hill, Charlie Scott, Dick Cottrell, Harry Gardner. *(Dorothy Ward)*

EMB employees' dinner at the Station Hotel, Dudley, *c.* 1951. Those on the top table include Elsie John, Norman John, George Cadbury, Robin Cadbury, Tim Cadbury, Stan Smith. Third table, left to right: Gladys Edmunds, Bert Edmunds, Olive Fieldhouse, George Barton, Len Hill. Second table: Hilda Chatwin, Ivor Aspley, Bert Penn, Harold Alltree, Lou Griffin, Vi Griffin, Harry Gardner. Front table: Doris Austin, Aubrey Austin, Frank Whitehouse, Jean Bayliss, Betty Welch, Dorothy Boyce, Josie Caldwell, George Morris, Nellie Morris, Des Allen, Betty Allen, Ivy Burns, Eric Medley. *(Dorothy Ward)*

The EMB football team, *c.* 1949. Back row, left to right: Harold Woodall, Harold Ward, Bernard Ward, Frank Guise, Dennis Woodall, Douglas Key, Tommy Bird, Len Agger. Front row: Harry Poulton, Harry Gardner, George Fox, Tommy Ward, Malcolm Lee. *(Dennis Woodall)*

Customers of the Turks Head, Sams Lane, pictured at the rear of the premises in about 1940 with what appears to be two mounted displays of coins. Back row, left to right: ? Beasley, -?-, ? Grinnell, Tom Thompson, -?-, Sam Roberts, -?-, Ed Beasley, ? Grinnell, Lesley Beasley. Middle row: -?-, -?-, Harold Fisher (licensee), Barbara Fisher, -?-, -?-, -?-. Front row: Bill Walsgrove, Joe Beards, -?-, -?-, Bert Beards, ? Grinnell, -?-, Bill Beasley. *(Sheila Walsgrove)*

St Michael Street looking towards New Street, 1967. A West Bromwich Corporation Weymann-bodied Daimler CVG6 bus en route to Oldbury is about to pass Underwood's Wines & Spirits premises on the corner of Paradise Street. In the background is the partly obscured YMCA building and *Midland Chronicle* newspaper office. *(Graham Harper)*

The High Street's junction with New Street (left) and St Michael Street, *c.* 1910. Drapers Dain & Morgan (left) were established in 1898 but between 1932 and 1968 these premises were used by Bell & Jones, chemist and photographic goods. Following the move to Queens Square in 1971 under the new ownership of D. & S. Peakman, the business, after seventy-two years in the town, was eventually taken over by The Image Store in December 2004. *(T.J.H. Price)*

Ronald D. Martin, better known as 'Ron Dicken', stands outside his immensely popular sports shop at 12 New Street before its closure in 1986. The firm, established in 1884 by John Horton Dicken at 52 New Street, relocated to No. 2 in 1890 and finally to No. 12, pictured above, in 1898. In 1932 the business was acquired by Albert William Martin who in 1948 was joined in the company by his son Ronald. The shop became known as Dicken Sports in about 1953. *(Ron Martin)*

The Palais de Danse, New Street, c. 1928. This extremely popular dance venue was established in 1926 by Emmanuel Samuel who also held boxing, wrestling and roller-skating here. After the Second World War it became better known as the Adelphi Ballroom, and it attracted crowds from all over the Midlands. In its heyday most of the top bands and pop groups performed there. It was a sad day for the town when fire destroyed the building on Sunday 23 May 1971. (T.J.H. Price)

This representation of a Robinsons (confectioners) Ltd shop front was constructed by Walter E. Tart, bakery manager and supervisor, for an arts and crafts exhibition held at West Bromwich Town Hall in January 1946. The display was arranged by Miss Ivy Commander, shop supervisor. William Robinson established the firm at 47 New Street in 1902 and at its peak had forty-five branches. When they closed on 28 January 1982 a number of their shops were taken over by Firkins. (David Tart)

The buildings in this section of New Street, photographed in May 1972, were demolished soon afterwards to make way for Cronehills Linkway. Noah Turner's Sandwell Garage on the right had already closed down along with John Allen & Son's radio, television and music shop. This latter company, however, continued trading from premises in Moor Street for a short while. John Allen was originally a pianoforte dealer on the High Street before moving to New Street in about 1945. (Geoff Hunt)

Sidney Darby & Son Ltd, 43 New Street, *c. 1972*. The business was established here in about 1908 after Sidney had taken over the property from Frederick Loach, a dairyman. From the outset Sidney was noted for the outstanding quality of his photographs which resulted in him being commissioned to cover many official events in the town. From 1954 the firm came under the control of Jack Darby before being acquired by Anthony Usherwood in 1980, the present owner. *(Charles Smith)*

New Street from Pitt Street looking towards Bratt Street (left), June 1969. The West Bromwich Corporation Daimler bus is just passing one of the town's oldest firms, Noah Turner Ltd, coal merchants of 25 Lombard Street and owners of Sandwell Garage pictured left. The Turner family had been associated with the coal industry since 1870 and with automobiles from 1919. *(Graham Harper)*

Messenger Lane looking towards Reform Street, *c.* 1965. Before New Street was extended early in the twentieth century this lane was a main access route to Dartmouth Park. Mayers Green Church was situated here until it was compulsorily purchased by the corporation in 1968. It was destroyed by fire in 1969. Finally, the lane disappeared completely when the new expressway cut through it in the early 1970s. *(Bob Spencer)*

Mayers Green Church drama group, winners of the Primary Challenge Trophy at the West Bromwich Drama Festival, 19 April 1947. Standing, from left to right: Ann Jones, Sylvia Jones, Doreen Knowles, Janet ?, Tony Legg, Olive Dicken, Madge Dicken, Roy Jones, June Woodall, Barbara ?, Pat Dicken. Seated, left: Frances Treadwell. *(Frances Davies)*

The Hen & Chickens, 52 Messenger Lane, pictured from Reform Street, March 1961. The landlords of this pub can be traced back more than 130 years with Thomas Biddlestone on record from 1834 to 1858. The Mason family appear also to have had a long association with it. William Mason was in charge here between 1866 and 1874, Emily Mason between 1874 and 1878, Arthur Mason from 1894 to 1918 and Ann Mason from 1918 to 1934. The last licensee before it closed on 8 June 1969 was Emily Yates. *(Sidney Darby & Son Ltd)*

Sandwell Public Works 'A' snooker team, Premier Division members of the West Bromwich League pictured in December 1974. From left to right: Carl Whitehouse, Keith Darby, Gordon Evans, Brendan Carless, Horace Gray, Terry Bonham. *(Pat Darby)*

West Bromwich Floral Queen Mary Richardson leaving the bandstand in Dartmouth Park after the crowning ceremony which was conducted by the Mayor, Cllr Minne Evitts, on 25 August 1961. Patricia Campbell was the Floral Queen's attendant. *(Mary Pattison)*

The crowning of the West Bromwich Horticultural Show Floral Queen Hazel Tinsley in Dartmouth Park by the Mayor, Alderman Ellen May Carpenter, on Saturday 26 August 1950.
From left to right: Yvonne Carpenter (Mayoress), Dorothy Smith, Hazel Tinsley (Floral Queen), Alderman Ellen May Carpenter (Mayor), Pamela Moorman, Cllr Harry Sower, -?-. *(Hazel Morris)*

The old and the new premises of Kenrick & Jefferson (right) dominate their surroundings in this 1938 view of the High Street. In 2002 the four-storey K & J building was demolished and replaced by the Astle Retail Park which to date has had little success. Note the iron railings in front of Lloyds Bank (extreme right) which were removed for the war effort in 1940. *(T.J.H. Price)*

Kenrick & Jefferson long service employees pictured in 1978. Those in the photograph include Mary Smith, Sylvia Wilkins, Irene Whitehouse, Madge Edwards, Rose Williams, Ivy Bellamy, Betty Richards, Les Dicken, Howard Smith, Gwen Perry, Eileen Slater, Winnie Partridge, Doug Smith, John Gray, Des Hickman, Ivan Walker, Frank Marston, Irene Waring, Florrie Mole, Lily Mallen, Gwen Rudge, Edna Poulton, Arthur Daniels, Sally Lord, Kathy Rock, Sid Wilkes, Ray Addis, Pat Smith, Ken Cadman, Vera Cooper, Vera Holyhead, Ron Massey, Tom Stokes. *(Lily Phillips)*

Donna Makepeace (left) and Lisa McFarland say hello to police horse Orchid at West Bromwich Police Station in 1984. The girls were members of the 2nd West Bromwich Brownies, based at Wesley Church, who were taking part in the National Brownie/Guide tea-making fortnight. The aim was to improve their tea-making skills. *(Betty Cooper)*

Wesley Church, High Street, Sunday School anniversary, *c.* 1949. Back row, left to right: Irene Saunders, Eileen Rowe, Terry Brown, John Cooper, Tony Legg, Arthur Newey. Among the fourth row: Vivien Ault, Margaret Warwick, Millie Newey, Janice Vickerstaff, Carol Holden, Janet Neale, Dorothy Wilkins. Third row: Jean Rowley, Audrey Harris, Michael Hawkes, Edward Legg, Ann Ryder, Judith Longbottom. Second row: Jean Smith, Pamela Whitehouse, Rosemary Newey, John Slater, Diane Chambers, Ann Wilkins, Ken Harris, Margaret Wall. Front row: Jeanette Hill, Mollie Neale, Barbara Dickins, Susan Taylor, Christine Ryder, Lynn Hawkes, Jean Wiggin, Kathleen Homeshaw. *(Beryl Price)*

Wesley Church, High Street, Sunday School anniversary, *c.* 1944. Back row, left to right: Dorothy Smith, Mary Palmer, Beryl Smith, Eve Cook, the Revd A. Simpson-Leck, Dorothy Wilkins, Mollie Bee, Irene Saunders. Third row: Barbara Greyer, ? Greyer, Douglas Cook, Beryl Thompson, Janice Vickerstaff, Margaret Warwick, Valerie Dyke, -?-, -?-, Diane Brierley. Second row: Vivien Ault, -?-, Millie Newey, Irene Walters, Derek Slater, ? Edwards, Margaret Smith. Front row: -?-, Edward Legg, -?-, Michael Alcock, -?-, Diane Chambers, -?-. *(Beryl Price)*

Wesley Church, High Street, Sunday School anniversary, *c.* 1958. In the pulpit is the Revd Handel Broadbent. Among the back row: Gillian Hancox, Jean Thompson. Third row: Murielle Smith, Beryl Thompson, Glynn Fieldhouse, Dorothy Smith, Eileen Rowe. Second row: Christine Ryder, Tessa Douglas, Ann Ryder, Irene Saunders. Front row: Jeanette Hill, Freda Hockley, Elizabeth Neale, Judith Overton, Elizabeth Fieldhouse, Jean Smith, Jean Brown. *(Beryl Price)*

Left: West Bromwich Gas showrooms decorated for the coronation of King George VI and Queen Elizabeth in May 1937. These premises, which were situated on the High Street next to the central library, were severely damaged as a result of an enemy bombing raid on the town during the evening of 19 November 1940. The frontage was demolished soon afterwards and new showrooms erected on the site. *(T.J.H. Price)*

Above: The Anchor public house, 303 High Street, *c.* 1948, when Harry Moseley was the licensee. Samuel Frier is shown on early records as the landlord between 1840 and 1870 but the pub's most famous tenant in 1902, before he moved to the Dartmouth Hotel in 1906, was West Bromwich Albion FC legend William Isaiah Bassett. Creswell's grocery shop premises next door now form part of the Anchor pub's lounge area. *(Andrew Maxam)*

Left: The Town Hall decorated for the coronation of King George VI and Queen Elizabeth in May 1937. An interesting feature of this building was architect William Henman's introduction of heating by ducts of warm air within the inside brickwork, the first of its kind in the world. The vents are still visible today. *(T.J.H. Price)*

Lower High Street and beyond, viewed from the top of the West Bromwich Technical College in 1962. Below, on the left, is the Baptist Church complete with its tower which was removed in 1967. The church closed in 1971 and was demolished the following year. A modern replacement was opened in Tantany Lane in 1974, the congregation having in the meantime used the Unitarian Church in Lodge Road. *(David Wilson)*

Jones & Co., gentlemen's outfitters and shirtmakers, 274 High Street, *c*. 1930. This business was established here in 1909 by hosier Robert William Jones after he acquired the property from Arthur Birch, a pianoforte dealer. In 1923, five years after Mary Ada Jones' succession, it became known as Jones & Co. Miss Tessa Jones and her mother Mary Ada then ran the business until its closure in 1966. *(Tessa Jones)*

Residents of Temple Street photographed from George Johnson's Royal Exchange pub, celebrating the coronation of Queen Elizabeth II, 2 June 1953. Among those pictured, from the back to the front row: Bill Jinks, Jack Fisher, Florence Crumpton, Lily Jinks, Dennis Knowles, Jack Thompson, Jack Willoughby, Rose Atkins, Muriel Whitehouse, Anne Willoughby, Sue Cooper, Florence Walker, Terry Waterhouse, Ivy Fisher, Joan Ogleby, Phyliss Cox, Lynn Emms, George Johnson (licensee), Kay Reader, Betty Reader, June Hobins, Beatrice Thompson, Jean Thompson, Beryl Thompson, Elizabeth Johnson, Geoffrey Reader, Madeline Thompson, Peter Andrews. *(Freda Johnson)*

George Mason Ltd, 377 High Street, corner of Shaftsbury Street, c. 1930. This grocery shop opened in 1923 and was one of almost five hundred operating throughout Britain. It is amazing that such a small branch could support so many members of staff. In 1950 the building was demolished and replaced with new offices for the adjoining Guest Motors Ltd. *(T.J.H. Price)*

The Old Hop Pole on the corner of High Street and Guns Lane, where it meets Carters Green, 2 August 1968. Wilfred Simson, the landlord at the time, holds the record for long service at this pub. He ran it from 6 October 1955 to 6 January 1972. Decoron Wallpapers' old shop at No. 470 is also shown, left of centre, as well as the Oddfellows Arms next door. Charles William Whitehouse was the licensee there. *(Alan Price)*

Carters Green looking towards the Farley Clock Tower and Methodist Church, *c.* 1930. In 1934 William Price, wireless engineer, of 6 Carters Green formed a partnership with Victor Bayliss. By 1938 the firm, then known as Price & Bayliss, had moved into the premises shown on the extreme left (No. 12). *(Jim Houghton)*

The Lodge Tavern, 140 Lodge Road, *c. 1922*. Pictured standing outside the premises are the landlord Walter Frederick Hilton and his wife Sophia, who remained here from 1922 to 1926. Curiously, between William Cox (1882–1902) and Harold Gillard (1942–56), the licence changed hands with striking regularity every four years. Following closure of the pub in 1988 the building was purchased by Peter Thomas who in April 2004 reopened it as a unisex hairdressing salon called Headstart. *(Peter Thomas)*

The Loving Lamb, 67 Dartmouth Street, *c. 1982*. The pub was just three years away from closure when this picture was taken. Archibald Simcox was the most well-known landlord, holding the licence for over fourteen years from 1926. Note the unusual bevelled corner of this building adjacent to Brook Street. *(T.J.H. Price)*

The Hop & Barleycorn, 57 Dartmouth Street, at the corner of Duke Street, *c. 1982*. Stanley North was another of the town's long-serving landlords, residing here for twenty-seven years from 8 January 1959 to 11 March 1986. The Bailey family had three of their number consecutively running this pub for twenty-eight years, Edward (1898–1902), Alice (1902–10) and Charles (1910–26). This ex-Joules house closed in 2004. *(T.J.H. Price)*

The Railway Inn, 79 Harwood Street, 2 August 1968, when Harriet Bevin was the landlady. Even in the days when public houses changed hands less frequently this one was a shining example of stability. During a fifty-six year period commencing 1906 only two families held the licence, Charles Morris (1906–26), his wife Mary Ann Morris (1926–34) and Leonard Dodd from 12 January 1933 to 4 January 1962. *(Alan Price)*

The all-conquering 'Champion of Champions' Darts Team of the Railway Inn, 79 Harwood Street, *c.* 1974. Left to right: Derek Hodgetts, John Hughes, -?-, Geoff Warner, Jimmy Joiner, Albert Finch, Jimmy Badhams, -?-, Colin Jennings, John Jones. Geoff Warner had the record of becoming the first player to win every match for two years running in the West Bromwich League, including remaining undefeated in all Staffordshire County Representative games. *(Ray Brookes)*

Nellie Stokes's High Class Fish & Chip Saloon, 16 Lambert Street, *c.* 1937. These premises were occupied in 1894 by William Stokes, a breeze dealer whose diverse business interests resulted in him becoming a grocer from 1904 to 1930 and a scrap metal merchant from 1930 to 1934. The building then became a fish and chip shop managed by Nellie Stokes until about 1939. From left to right: Nellie Stokes, Kate Baker, Winifred Taylor. *(Marjorie Welham)*

The visit of Jack Martze, American evangelist, to West Bromwich Town Hall, *c.* 1947. Representatives from all churches in the town attended the event which was led by Pastor Rees J. Griffiths. From left to right: Clem Llewellyn, Les Robinson (both facing away), Claudia Griffiths, Pastor Rees J. Griffiths, Jack Martze, Renée Martze, Mrs J. Martze, Ruby May James, Pastor Byatt, Cliff Nicholls (at the piano). *(Sid Haynes)*

Right: Carter's fish and chip shop, 22 Chapman Street, *c.* 1928. These premises were originally used as a general store by David Cattell in 1898 followed by Sidney George Middlestone from 1906 to 1910, Sarah Basford from 1910 to 1914 and Bob Reed from 1914. It eventually became a fish and chip shop in 1924 when Elizabeth Carter took over. She continued the business until 1950 when it was sold to James and Annie Woodhall. On the doorstep are Vera Carter and Wilfred Medley. *(Dennis Carpenter)*

Above: Lydia Ward, clothing and wardrobe dealer, 25 Old Meeting Street, *c.* 1910. This business appears to have been of short duration, lasting from 1910 until about 1915. The family had other commercial interests, however, with Charles Ward having a bricklaying concern at 102 Oak Road. From left to right: Charles Ward, Lydia Sarah Banks Ward, Edith Ward, Violet Ward, Agatha Ward, Arthur Ward. *(Hazel Morris)*

Right: Nellie Ralphs stands in the doorway of Ralphs bakery and shop at 29 Carters Green, *c.* 1930. George Genner, earthenware dealer, was an early occupant of these premises from 1870 to 1882 followed by grocer Henry Gardner from 1882 to 1890. William Holloway later added a bakery before selling the business to Thomas Ralphs in 1902. Leonard Ralphs became the registered owner between 1926 and about 1982 after which the property was sold to Swinton Insurance. *(Robert Ralphs)*

Carters Green, looking towards Lower High Street, March 1939. This view has the unusual sight of a Birmingham Corporation tramcar passing a double-decker bus on the same No. 74 route. This 'special' was probably on a test run as buses did not take over this service until after the trams had ceased on 1 April 1939. *(Jim Houghton)*

The interior of Martin's confectionery and tobacconist shop, 61 Carters Green, showing Gay Martin and shop assistant Barbara Powell behind the counter, *c.* 1956. *Kelly's Trade Directory* of 1872 shows a grocery business at this address under the ownership of Hester Kebby and from 1882 onwards it was a tobacconists with confectionery being added only after John Martin had acquired the property in 1922. *(Sheila Swan)*

Carters Green from Dudley Street, 20 July 1968. On the left is a side view of the gothic-style Wesleyan Methodist Church, built on the site of the old Junction Inn in 1875/76 to a design by the Loxton brothers of Wednesbury. After closing in about 1949 it was used for some years as a warehouse before being demolished in 1970. (*Alan Price*)

West Bromwich Amateurs FC pictured at the Hawthorns in 1952 before playing Furnace Sports in the final of the Albion Shield. West Bromwich Amateurs were also runners-up in Division 1A of the Handsworth League and winners of the Oldbury Charity Cup. Back row, left to right: Sam Sims, J. Caddick, Gordon Stockin, Reg Homer, Des Holloway, Ted Powell, Edgar Lawton, Jim Hodgetts. Middle row: Cliff ?-, Joe Tillitson, Ray Markham (captain), Bill Webb, Eric Jones, -?-. Front row: Fred Francis, Tom Cutler. (*Ray Markham*)

Dudley Street, with the Nags Head public house on the right, *c.* 1930. This was the main route of the London–Holyhead coaches during the eighteenth century before improvements made at Holloway Bank enabled them to be re-routed through Wednesbury. An original milestone in use during this period can still be seen today, just before Cordley Street on the left. *(Jim Houghton)*

Hayes United FC, Division 1 members of the West Bromwich & District Sunday League, 1964/65. Back row, left to right: Ray Shelley, John Simcox, Arthur Brown, Alan Shepherd, Brian Walford, Harry Rose, Derek Graham, Jim Simcox. Front row: Mick 'Jack' Payne, George Ralph, Barry Hackett, Len Ralph, Mick Richards. *(Harry Rose)*

The Horseshoe FC, *c.* 1965, a member of the West Bromwich & District Sunday League Division 1. Back row, left to right: John ?, 'Mac' McCloud, Martin Duncombe, Derrick Davies, Keith Knight, David Bishop, Phil Whitehouse, David John. Front row: Mike O'Gorman, Steve Day, Mel Kent, Mick Plant, Ron Windsor. *(Mel Kent)*

West Bromwich licensed victuallers' annual dinner, the New Inns, Handsworth, 1950. In the back row: Joe Worrall, Florence Dodd, Ellen May Carpenter (Mayor of West Bromwich), Fred Everiss, Leonard Dodd, Arthur Tomlinson. Table 'F', left to right, near side: Eddie Davies, Harold Wall, Albert Woodward, Harry Griffiths, Bill Finney, -?-, Sam Cooper, -?-, George Harris, Jack Wall, Arthur Knowles. Far side: Ted Woodward, Arthur Cole, Gibian Bates, Ike Bradley, Frank Longmore, Fred Aston, Bill Mercer, -?-, Tom Knight, Jack Male, Gordon Whitehouse, Ken Hamilton. Second table: Harry Reynolds. *(Iris Reynolds)*

Residents of Tyndal Street, Carters Green line up in front of John Street for an egg and spoon race during celebrations marking the coronation of Queen Elizabeth II on 2 June 1953. From left to right: -?-, -?-, -?-, Lucy Lewis, Lucy Firkin, Gwen Moore, Betty Simcox, -?-, Freda Jones, May Edge Snr, -?-, -?-, Annie Grice, Michael Jones, May Edge Jnr. In the background are the premises of Hill-Robinson Ltd, mechanical engineers and ironfounders, who were established here in 1930. *(Gordon Parker)*

Old Meeting Street viewed from outside George Hill's Motor Coach Tours premises, looking towards Carters Green, *c.* 1968. Crates of beer are being unloaded from one of three Ansells brewery vehicles parked outside the Inkerman Cottage public house on the left. Joseph Thomas Connor was the landlord at this time, and also when it closed on 9 December 1968. The pub was given the name Inkerman to celebrate victory in a battle which took place on 5 November 1854 during the Crimean War. The Russians, under the command of Prince Menshikov, were defeated by the Franco-British troops under Lieutenant General the Earl of Raglan. *(Geoff Williams)*

Young Tories taking part in the 1953 West Bromwich Carnival pictured aboard a decorated Wellington Tube Works lorry driven by Charles Smith. The dinosaur-themed float is approaching Carters Green from Old Meeting Street where many in the crowd have secured a vantage point on the Wesleyan Chapel in the background. *(Frank Smith)*

Chapter Three

Black Lake, Great Bridge, Greets Green & Swan Village

Ex-Wolves and England soccer captain Billy Wright pictured in the die-casting department of Great Bridge Foundry Ltd, Sheepwash Lane Great Bridge, *c.* 1960. Billy was employed in a representative capacity by the firm for a short period following his retirement from playing professional football in August 1959. From left to right: -?-, -?-, Arthur Harrison, Billy Wright, Beryl Paskin, Winnie ?. *(Aubrey Hudson)*

The firm of Alfred Ellison Ltd, iron founders, Black Lake Works, Swan Lane, was established in about 1926 and had 200 workers at its peak. Some of them are pictured here in 1935. Among those on the photograph: George Abel, ? Bant, ? Broadbent, Tom Blackford, Harry Creswell. Front row: Sammy Matthews, -?-, -?-, Frank Blackford, Fred Blackford, -?-, -?-, -?-, -?-, -?-, David Blackford, -?-, -?-, -?-. *(Heather Whitehouse)*

Employees of Hall & Rice Staffordshire Wire Mill, Small Street, Black Lake, celebrating the forthcoming wedding of colleague Graham Tarr in 1961. Back row, left to right: Lloyd Parsons, Brian Beard, Frank Wall, Dennis Hill, Billy Walker, Charlie Knott, Ken Kilvert, David Mannion, Ray Vowles, Arthur Broomhall. Front row: Ernie Wheatley, John Beckett, Richard Curtis, Geoff Stevens, Tom Whitehouse, Graham Tarr, Charlie Walker. *(Graham Tarr)*

The Queen's Head, 101 Church Lane, Black Lake, November 1933. This pub's licence was held for over forty years by the Sperring family: firstly by George (1906–14) and then by Bert from 1914 onwards. Private houses have recently replaced the industrial property shown on the left while the wasteland on the right is now Small Street. *(Andrew Maxam)*

Steel Parts Ltd, Brickhouse Lane, Great Bridge, executive and staff dinner held at the New Inns, Handsworth on 18 April 1952. Near table, right side: Ray Garrett, -?-, Dennis Bell, -?-, Arthur Hensman, Lily Moseley, -?-, -?-, Fred Overton, -?-. Left side: Doris Sheldon, -?-, Doreen Bell, -?-, Marion Hensman, -?-, -?-, George Sherwood, Winnie Overton, -?-. Among those on the second table: Edna Webster, Bill Tranter, Stan Wilkins, Harry Bates, John Morgan, Joan Wilkins. *(Doreen Bell)*

Wellington Tube Works, Brickhouse Lane Great Bridge, netball team, *c.* 1947. They were winners of the Barlow Cup after defeating Spon Lane in the final, 11–9. Back row, left to right: Meryl Waldron, Betty Coles, Rita Dovey, Violet Basford. Front row: Mary Adams, Winifred Shelton, Gillian Hopkins. *(Tom Shelton)*

Great Bridge, at the junction of Whitehall Road (left), *c.* 1964. The Victor Value supermarket (centre) was taken over by Tesco in 1967 but they too were to move out thirteen years later. The building is now a branch of Total Do-It-Yourself Ltd. Civic Radio's shop eventually became Preedy's News & Tobacconist but since 1990 it has been better known as The Papershop, owned and managed by Jim Cheema. *(Edwin Yates)*

Shops numbered 5 to 17 Great Bridge pictured in 1980 awaiting demolition, with the area destined to become an extended car park for the nearby market hall. In February 2004 a controversial plan to build sixty homes on the site was approved by Sandwell planners despite protest petitions claimed to have been signed by almost 3,000 people. *(Frank Wardle)*

Employees of the Wellington Tube Works, Great Bridge, who received awards for twenty-five years' service, *c.* 1962. Back row, left to right: Bill Turner, ? Pedley, Arthur ?, Bill Whale, George Whitehouse. Middle row: Jack Cleary, Ted Nuttall, Albert Austin, Ray Dickin, Ray ?. Front row: Billy Williams, William Beasley, Harry Howes, Douglas Turner, Charles Tranter, -?-, -?-. *(George Whitehouse)*

The Plough & Harrow, 89 William Street, Great Bridge, with licensees Tom and Elizabeth Jane Withington standing on the doorstep, *c.* 1925. Tom and Elizabeth went on to become the pub's longest tenants with thirty-four years' service from 1910. These premises were owned by the Wolverhampton-based Frank Myatt's Brewery who sold out to Holts in 1927. Seven years later, in 1934, Holts Brewery were themselves taken over by Ansells Ltd. When the street became the subject of a clearance order in the late 1960s the Plough & Harrow was one of the last buildings to be demolished. William Street was also the home of that well-known and loveable character Bertie Amos, before he moved to Westminster Road Stone Cross. His passion for following steamrollers and 'driving' buses all over West Bromwich is legend. *(Linda Darby)*

VE Day celebrations in Elwell Street, Great Bridge, 8 May 1945. Among the crowd, from left to right: Doreen Worley, Doreen Markham, Jeff Stampe, Violet Vaughan, Sarah Hunt, Bertie Wilkins, Olive Baker, Olwyn Gilson, Dickie Taylor, June Taylor, Margaret Hartshorne, Geoff Cox, Arthur Worley, Ray O'Brien, Jack Baker, Len Markham, Cliff Markham, Gordon Taylor, Gordon Hoult, Brenda Cox, Joe Markham, Albert Markham, Mary Ward, Tommy Fellows, Alf Gilson, Ruth Stampe, Ernie Markham. *(Olwyn Dyke)*

Employees of Brade-Leigh Products Ltd, commercial motor body builders, Great Bridge, *c.* 1945. Back row, left to right: Horace Francis, Ron Hadley, -?-, Ron Bevan, -?-, -?-, Joe Hughes, Tommy Parsons, Jim Lee. Middle row: Bert Yates, Cyril Evans, Sam Peplow, Jim Shadwell, Brian Bradley, -?-, -?-, Stan Pottinger, -?-,-?-, -?-, -?-, Frank 'The Sweep' ?, Jim Hyde. Seated: Edward G. Bradley, Iris Ashmore, Henry Bradley, Harry Bradley, Vera Price, Ken Millington. *(Iris Brown)*

Crowds of children gather outside Charles Purser's post office on the corner of Brickhouse Lane, Great Bridge during the early part of the nineteenth century to witness the approach of a recently introduced electric tramcar. When this picture postcard was published in 1903 as part of the Wrench Series it was among the first to have been printed in colour. *(Ken Rock)*

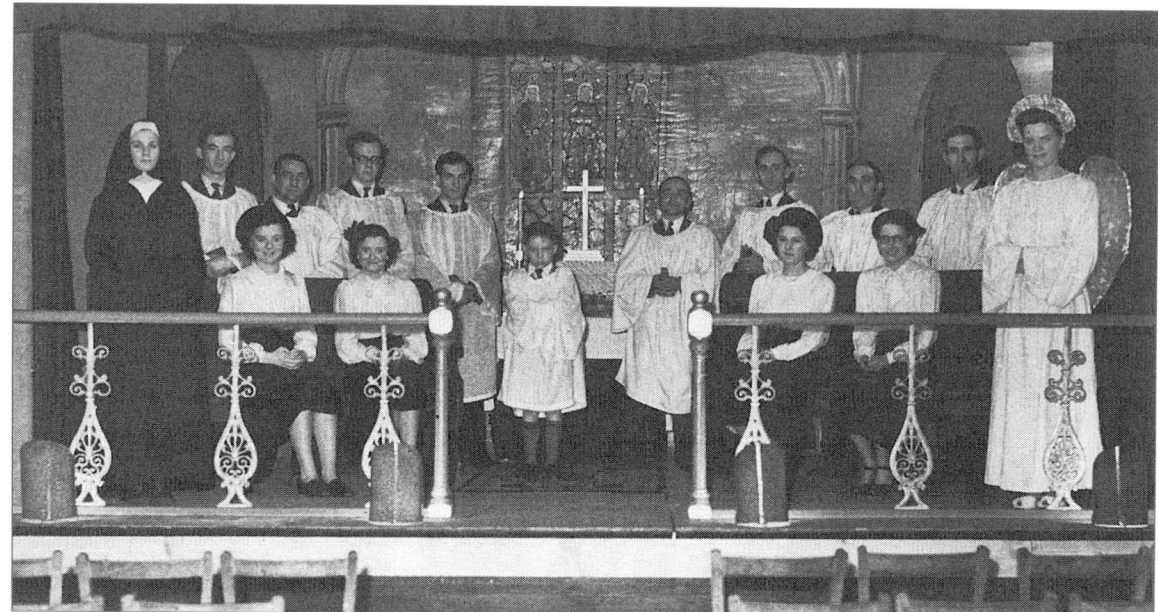

Songs with a church theme performed by the Optimists concert party of Salem Church, Sheepwash Lane, Great Bridge, *c.* 1952. Back row, left to right: Douglas Brevitt, Cliff Williams, Len Markham, Gordon Brevitt, Alan Ball, Cliff Ball, Manny Wright, Horace Parkes, Claude York. Front row: Brenda Steventon, Margaret Whitehouse, Brenda Whitehouse, Brenda Williams, Gladys Whitehouse, Jean Roberts. *(Pat Hickman)*

The Christian Spiritualist Church situated in Whitehall Road, opposite Farley Street, Great Bridge, June 1959. The lower part of this building was originally two shops, Mrs Coley's fruiterers (left) and Robinsons confectioners (right). The church at that time conducted their services on the upper floor with Mr Stackhouse and Hannah Taylor among the mediums. By 1970 the property was no longer in use and had become derelict. *(Ron Jones)*

Off-duty police officers pictured behind the bar of the Royal Oak in Whitehall Road, Great Bridge, *c.* 1957. This 'investigation' is being observed on the right by the pub's licensees, Ted and Ann Penny. From left to right: Detective Sergeant Frank Woolley, Jack Hughes, Detective Constable Bill Moore, -?-. Background: -?-. *(Royal Oak)*

St Peter's Church festival procession seen in Whitehall Road, Great Bridge, during their 1921 May Day celebrations. The vicar at the time was the Revd Frank Smith who was succeeded at St Peter's in 1925 by the very popular and long-serving Revd Lancelot John Lamplugh. *(Alan Price)*

These two amazing pictures show a float preparing to take part in the West Bromwich carnival of 1928 with two people dressed as members of the Ku Klux Klan, a secret organisation of white protestant Americans. Kingfisher Ltd, school furniture manufacturers of Charles Street, Great Bridge, entered this tableaux bearing the name 'The Bored School', bored being a pun on the word Board. This magnificent vehicle is parked in Old Meeting Street outside the offices of Charles Adams & Sons, oil merchants. *(Linda Darby)*

School desktop workers pictured on No. 2 factory roof at (ESA) Kingfisher Ltd in Charles Street, Great Bridge, c. 1974. Back row, left to right: Tony Jukes, Roy Jones. Third row: Mike Secker, Bill Nightingale, Terry Jones, Mike Boyes. Second row : Lenny Eccleston, -?-, Stan Yates, Geoff Bryant. Front row: Malcolm Jacks, Geoff Charnock, David ?. (Colin Boyes)

Greets Green, from Greets Green Road with Oldbury Road left, Whitehall Road ahead and Ryders Green Road on the right, 18 January 1975. In the centre of the picture is a WMPTE Daimler CVG6/30 Metro-Cammell Orion-bodied bus on the No. 20 Stone Cross to Gough Arms service via Albion, Dartmouth Square and Heath Lane. This area was decimated in the late 1960s and early '70s when almost all of the shops, pubs and the school building were demolished. (David Wilson)

The 8th West Bromwich Boys' Brigade football squad based at Ryders Green Methodist Church, c. 1965. Back row, left to right: Manohar Patel, Ken Holt, David Cooksey, Vinod Patel, Michael Steventon, John Briscoe, Alan Farrington. Middle row: -?-, Michael Flynn, John Lowe, David Newey, -?-. Front row: Robert Parkes, Kevin Millward, Michael Smith, -?-. (Dennis Woodall)

An Evergreens production of *Mother Goose* at Greets Green Primitive Methodist Church, *c.* 1938. Back row, left to right: Vera Pitt, Joyce Dixon, Joan Tandy, Vera Poulton, Malcolm Cooke, Norman Fieldhouse, Sidney Fletcher, Norman Lester, Olga Bayley, Annie Dyke, Marjorie Fieldhouse, Horace Watton, Ivy Round. Right group: Dorothy Carter, Jean Arnold, Doreen Whitehouse, Irene Miller. Second row: Doreen Lester, Irene Benger, June Magee, Marjorie Tudor. Front row: Doreen Cox, Olive Bott, Vida Round, Joan Miller, Bobby Arnold, Joyce Miller, -?-, Alice Watton, Brenda Arnold. *(Olive Ellis)*

Jack & Jill presented by the Evergreens, *c.* 1962. Back row, left to right: Michael Vaughan, Geoff Robinson, Sid Wright, Beryl Martin. Middle row: Graham Dyke, Maureen Smith, Valerie Woodcock, Anne Round, Jacqueline Joyce, Dorothy Manders, Sheila Whitehouse, Colin Gadd, Ivy Round. Front row: Janet Bishop, Pauline Scragg, Barbara Smith, Gillian Geddes, Diane Vaughan, Linda Thompson, Maureen Watson, Clive Westwood, Angela Westwood, -?-. *(Maureen Lippitt)*

Sleeping Beauty performed by the Evergreens, 1952. Back row, left to right: Jean Earpe, Eunice Carpenter, Sid Wright, Howard Baker, Maurice Poulton, -?-, Stan Dodd, Derek Cadd, Bill Colley, David Wilding, Ron Barker, Shirley Icke, -?-, Pat Randle, -?-. Fourth row: Brian Beckett, John Ralph, Barry Hopson, Beryl Timmins, Ivy Round. Third row: Shirley Newell, Tony Welch, John Smith, Beatrice Dodd, Hazel Jackson, Joan Smith, Beryl Woolley, Janet Reynolds, -?-, Linda Plevey. Second row: Douglas Cook, Barbara Smith, Norman Bunn. Front row: Madeleine Icke, Janice Lucas, Gwen Woolley, Janet Thomas, Anne Round, Sheila Grinnell, Maureen Smith, Pauline Scragg, Norma Law, Graydon Summers. *(Tony Welch)*

The Evergreens' 1948 pantomime, *Babes in the Wood*. Back row, left to right: Dorothy Cooksey, Olive Spink, Brenda Arnold, Jean Beddow, Dorothy Fellows, Irene Vipond, Iris Howes, Beryl Whitehouse. Front row: Joan Smith, Ann King, Janet Thomas, Janice Lucas, Cynthia Nutt, Diane Winchurch, Margaret George, Sheila Grinnell, -?-, Barbara Arnold, Sheila Doughty. In the centre is Ann Bridges. *(Maureen Lippitt)*

Sandwell Dresden FC, Division 6 winners of the Sandwell Sunday League, players presentation evening attended by ex-Albion and England centre forward Derek Kevan, 1980/81. Back row, left to right: Gary Roberts, Carl Hunter, Derry Campbell, Terry Purcell, Dean Wallburn, Tyrone Bratt, Ivan Bratt, Brian Rowe, Errol Douglas, Derek Kevan, Mick Reed, David Higgins, Bill Sharratt, Kevin Bratt. *(David Higgins)*

The Bush Inn, Wood Lane, with Claypit Lane on the left, March 1961. The pub which previously stood on this site dates from about 1845, the name 'Bush' also being used at that time by the nearby Bush Farm Colliery owned by Samuel Downing. When this picture was taken the landlord was Leslie Edward Perry but his predecessor, Harry Reynolds, is better remembered. The inn closed in 2001 when part of it was converted into flats. The building is now a community centre. *(Sidney Darby & Son Ltd)*

Customers of the Bush Inn, Wood Lane, enjoying a pint in the lounge, *c.* 1960. Back row standing, left to right: Alan James, Geoff Perry, Horace 'Oscar' Jones. Middle row: David Holland, Geoff Raybould, Gordon Mills, Billy Dangerfield, Malcolm Durran. Front row, right side: Maurice Pritchard, Jack Hartley, Roy Matthews. *(Jimmy Badhams)*

The Bush and Charlemont Star FC, after their 2–2 draw in the final of the Les Cobb Memorial Shield, 11 May 1966. Back row, left to right: Gordon Longhurst, Tony Rzepkowski, Michael Secker, Gordon Lee, Paul Roberts, Frank Griffiths, Fred Smith, Keith Rzepkowski, John Charlton, Brian Perry, Bob Langford, Mike Aspbury, Sid Davies, David Livingstone. Middle row: Trevor Roberts, Graham Brookes, John Cole, Cliff Hedges, Trevor Garman, Bobby Hadley. Front row: -?-, Ray Newell, -?-, Fred Woodcock, Geoff Green, John Powell. *(Garth Thomas)*

Rudge Littley darts team, winners of Division B in the Greets Green League, 1949/50. Back row, left to right: -?-, Joe Lambert, Joe Coley, -?-, Joe Hunt, -?-. Front row: Frank Webb, -?-, George Evans, -?-. This firm of ironfounders was originally established in Birmingham and moved here to Phoenix Street, Swan Village in 1914. The business closed in 2001. *(Linda Darby)*

During the Second World War, many of the firms in the industrialised areas of Britain found it essential to have their own means of extinguishing fires following bombing raids. Consequently, Rudge Littley Ltd, ironfounders of Phoenix Street, Swan Village, formed their own auxiliary fire brigade pictured here in 1941. From left to right: Harold Hunt, Ben Bailey, Arthur Capewell, -?-. *(Bob Arnold)*

Swan Village junction looking towards Great Bridge and the distant Ocker Hill power station cooling towers, *c.* 1950. This Dudley branch ran alongside the main Paddington–Birkenhead line at this point with the adjacent station building, opened to passengers in November 1854 and closed in March 1972, just visible on the right. *(Stations UK)*

Swan Village, looking towards Dudley Street with Phoenix Street on the right, 25 March 1973. This area is totally unrecognisable today with every building in the picture having disappeared in a reorganisation of the road layout. Swan Village Methodist Church, pictured centre, held a dedication service of restoration on Saturday 1 September 1962 following work to reduce the height of the building. The church closed in April 1987. *(Alan Price)*

Swan Village Methodist Church Round 'O' concert party performing in the schoolroom, *c.* 1952. Terence Stott is second from the left in the back row with Gwen Franks first on the left, middle row. Front row, with the top hat, is Roland Hollyhead. Left side, front to back: Blanche Hollyhead, Peter Geary, Margaret Morgan, -?-, -?-, June Hooper, -?-, -?-. On the right side row, third from the front, is Mavis Stott. *(Margaret Morgan)*

Swan Village Homing Society 5 Bird Club, individual prize winners, season 1963. From left to right: Joe Sheldon (chairman), Joe Mills (combined average), William Jones (secretary/young bird average), D. Taylor (old bird inland average), Joe Shakespeare (secretary of Dudley & District Federation of Flying Clubs), Jim Chamberlain (President of Dudley & District Federation of Flying Clubs), Douglas Ken Mullaney (premier prize winner). *(Ken Mullaney)*

Swan Village Gas Works first aid team during a training session, *c.* 1965. Even before the Health & Safety Act of 1974 the firm was always very forward thinking in this respect and took the safety and well-being of its employees very seriously indeed. From left to right: Teddy Brown, Reg Chamberlain, Gordon Taylor, Jim Aston, -?-. *(Ann Taylor)*

Children of Swan Village Gas Works employees enjoying themselves at a Christmas party held in the canteen, *c.* 1957. Only three children on the photograph can be identified, second table, front row: -?-, -?-, Edward Marsden, Barbara Marsden, Amy Marsden. *(Amy Budworth)*

A superb array of home-made Easter bonnets displayed by members of the Gas Club, Swan Village Gas Works, *c.* 1968. Back row, left to right: -?-, -?-, Margaret Darling, Florence Poynton, ? Grigg, Alice Houghton, Margaret Sargent, Joan ?, Irene Long. Front row: -?-, Rebecca Bullivant, Elsie Pitt, Lucy Page, Irene Baker, -?-, ? Long, -?-. *(Margaret Sargent)*

Right: Shunters Ted Marsden (left) and Ozzie Hunt (right) photographed with their 0–4–0 DH four-wheel diesel hydraulic locomotive in Swan Village Gas Works, August 1966. This shunting engine was built in 1960 by the North British Locomotive Company of Glasgow and had a works number of NBL-C27544. It was modified by Andrew Barclay Ltd in 1964 and was in service at Swan Village between 1964 and 1967. *(Amy Budworth)*

James Downing's original Yew Tree Inn, Albion Road, 8 June 1974. This photograph was taken just two days before the nearby replacement premises opened, with Francis Thomas Cox as the licensee. Samuel Downing, a local landowner during the early nineteenth century, was the first landlord, and he handed it over to his son James in 1874. Interestingly, there was still a James Downing holding the licence over sixty-five years later. *(Alan Price)*

An outing to Worcester from the Birco Motor Cylinder Co. of 119 Oak Road, pictured outside the Oak House in about 1936, shortly before the firm transferred its operation to Oldbury Road, Greets Green. Among those awaiting departure are Edward Collins, Arthur Fletcher, Alfred Collins, Harry Collins, Bill Taylor, Bill Collins. *(Sheila Haynes)*

Chapter Four

Golds Hill, Hall End, Hateley Heath & Hill Top

Percy Alfred Oswin, high class butcher, 29 Hawkes Lane, Hill Top, *c.* 1954. The business was acquired by Percy in 1934 from William Nightingale who at that time was trading at 6 Hawkes Lane. By 1936 Percy Oswin had also opened the premises pictured above, which had previously been a tailors run by John and Benjamin Purslow. In 1945, following Percy's death, Maud Oswin took over and assisted by Fred Bartram she continued the business until the shop closed in 1966. On the doorstep are Fred Bartram and Maud Oswin. *(Fred Bartram)*

Members of Hall End Methodist Church taking part in the West Bromwich Carnival, *c.* 1951. Back row, left to right: Sheila Aspley, Geoffrey Faulkner, Alan Powell, -?-, Albert Taylor, Alex Darling, -?-, Marion Ceney, Doreen Knowles, -?-, Maureen Coker, Bill Richards, -?-, David Rowley, Pauline Dunn, Sandra Kendrick, Sheila Clarke, Gwen Slater, Pat Slater, Margaret 'Peggy' Guy, Gladys Taylor, -?-. Front row: -?-, -?-, Paul Davies, Ben Slater, Dennis Richards, Pat Waite, -?-. *(Evelyn Farmer)*

The sixty-fourth Hall End Methodist Sunday School anniversary parade awaiting departure in Vicarage Road, June 1966. Among those in the procession, front to back: Annette Hill, Kim Keeling, Julie Denigan, Sandra Thompson, Gillian Edwards, Evelyn Farmer, Jean Rowley, Pauline Daniels, Pauline Slater, Anita Smith. On the pavement, left: Geoff Smith; right: Hilda Richards. *(Irene Thompson)*

The Mayor and Mayoress of West Bromwich, Cllr Joshua Churchman and his wife Violet, visit Hall End Methodist Church to present children with Sunday School anniversary prizes, 23 October 1966. Back row, left to right: Cllr Joshua Churchman, Wendy Harris, Beverley Bowen, Annette Hill, Sandra Thompson, Julie Denigan, Gillian Edwards, Violet Churchman. Front row: -?-, Helen Predotta, -?-. Seated, right: Florence Cotterell. *(Irene Thompson)*

Hall End Methodist Sunday School anniversary, *c.* 1970. Back row, left to right: Margaret Smith, Annette Hill, Gillian Edwards, -?-, Julie Denigan, Ian Hadley, -?-, -?-, Sandra Thompson, -?-, Sylvia Proctor. Third row, first on right: Cheryl Cartwright. Second row, first and ninth from the left: Diane Terry, Helen Predotta. Front row: Vera Davies, Ivy Timmins, Stephen Thompson, Audrey Millward, -?-, -?-, -?-, -?-, -?-, -?-, Anna ?, Joan Cartwright. *(Irene Thompson)*

Girls Life Brigade and Lifeboys leading the Sunday School anniversary procession of Hall End Methodist Church along Wiltshire Way/Rutland Road, Hateley Heath, *c.* 1961. Among the Girls Life Brigade, from left to right: Sandra Kendrick, Irene Nightingale, Kathleen Treadwell, Jeanette Norton, Elizabeth Greatbatch, Christine Predotta, Carol Kershaw, Carol Read, Judith Sowry, Diane Goodby, Hazel Faulkner, Margaret Guy. On the pavement, right: Harold Gore, the Revd John Beech. Following behind: Keith Slater, Alex Darling. *(Kathleen Hall)*

The Hall End Tavern (Ramper Tamper), 114 Vicarage Road, *c.* 1968, when William Wade was the licensee. These premises were built in about 1934 to replace an older property opposite, occupied by the Horton family between 1898 and about 1918. The new pub was originally owned by William Butler & Co. before passing to Mitchells & Butlers, Bass and the present owners, Punch Taverns. *(T.J.H. Price)*

Hall End Methodist Church Sunday School anniversary, 1952. Back row, first, second, sixth, tenth, twelfth from the left: Pat Waite, Pam Sowry, Sheila Mountford, Sheila Clarke, Paul Davies. Sixth row, tenth, eleventh, fourteenth: Maureen Howes, Maureen Coker, Geoffrey Faulkner. Fifth row, fourth, tenth, thirteenth: Sandra Kendrick, Pat Slater, Alan Powell. Fourth row: fourteenth, fifteenth, seventeenth: Alex Darling, Kenneth Clarke, David Rowley. Second row, eighth, tenth, eleventh, fourteenth: Hazel Faulkner, Betty Rushton, Kathleen Treadwell, Valerie Clarke. Among the front row: Ann Boylin, Freda Smith, Mary Boylin, Maureen Watts, John Watts, Keith Lake. *(Kathleen Hall)*

The Junction Inn Angling Club, Witton Lane, Hill Top, prize presentation evening held at the Hateley Heath Working Mens Club, *c.* 1970. Back row, left to right: Melvin Stackhouse, Micky Plant, George Ayres, -?-, Billy Foster. Front row: Harry Dent, Graham Tarr, Des Stanton, Teddy Cooper. *(Graham Tarr)*

Here's a sight you don't see very often these days: pigs being reared in a back garden, 1951. They were eventually sold to butchers Charles and Fred Quance of High Street, West Bromwich. The two ladies looking into the sty, at the rear of 21 Somerset Road, Hateley Heath, are Catherine 'Kit' Treadwell (left) and Frances Treadwell. *(Frances Davies)*

Hateley Heath Working Men's Club in-house sports presentation evening, *c.* 1975. Back row, left to right: Alan Winsper, John Watton, Ken Pratt, George Yates. Middle row: Ernie Watson, Ken Tarr, Sam Holmer, Terry Simmons, Graham Tarr, Vic Langford. Front, crouching: Colin Evans. *(Graham Tarr)*

The Coach & Horses, 33 Kesteven Road, Hateley Heath, *c.* 1964. Leslie Horace Knight was the landlord at the time of this picture and also on record as the first. His occupancy lasted from 8 January 1959 until 25 July 1968 making him the longest-serving so far. In 1998 the pub's name was changed to the Moon Under Water by new owners J.D. Wetherspoon plc, but has since reverted to its original name. *(Andrew Maxam)*

Hateley Heath WMC FC, Division 3 runners-up in the West Bromwich Sunday League and winners of the C.T. Richards Cup, season 1962/63. Back row, left to right: Jim Aspbury, Sid Roden, Peter Jeavons, Bob Weston, Charlie Botfield, Trevor Weston, Bob Jakeways, Ben Banner, Bill Davies. Front row: Micky White, David Knight, Barry Guest, Graham Tarr, Sam Richards, John Chatterton, David Cheese, George Banner. *(Graham Tarr)*

Wolseley Road, Harvills Hawthorn, celebrating the coronation of Queen Elizabeth II, 2 June 1953. Back row, left to right: -?-, -?-, -?-, -?-, Harold Devey. Middle row: -?-, -?-, Evelyn Shenston, Freda Harris, Elsie Law, ? Maybury, -?-, -?-, Brenda Steventon, -?-, Edmund Devey, Gladys Devey. Front row: Maureen Shelley, Edith Hodgkins, Doreen Maul, Betty Bowen (holding Linda Bowen), Annie Maul, Dora Smith (holding Susan Bowen), Mary Steventon, Barbara Smith. *(Sandra Bird)*

Albert George Ball's new corner grocery stores, 53–5 St Vincents Crescent, 6 October 1952. The shop is now Mo's Food and Wine Store. The business was established by Albert at 71 Dial Lane in 1934 and continued there until it closed in 1956. By this time the remaining part of Harvills Hawthorn No. 1 estate was being completed, which was to have a positive effect on this shop's future prospects. *(Annie Ball)*

The Britannia Inn, 119 Dial Lane, October 1962. Henry Saunders was the licensee at this time and was destined to take over the replacement premises which can be seen nearing completion on the left. The Britannia's licence was transferred to the new pub on 15 November 1962 and the opening took place ten days later. *(Alan Nicholls)*

St Paul's Church, Golds Hill, Sunday School anniversary parade approaching from Harvills Hawthorn and about to pass Reg Jackson's post office and grocery shop on the right, June 1951. Around the banner, from left to right: Ben Allsop, Walter Sharman, William Andrews, Gordon Castle, Trevor Beech, Joe Williams. *(Albert Murphy)*

A visit to Josiah Wedgwood & Sons Ltd, Barlaston, from St Paul's Church, Golds Hill, *c.* 1965. Back row, left to right: -?-, -?-, Edna Aston, Muriel Jones. Fourth row: -?-, ? Hassell, Ethel Simcox, Gwen Fellows, -?-, Ruth Boden, ? Priddy. Third row: Marge O'Kelly, Betty Ridler, Mary Murphy, Milly Suffolk, -?-, John Boden. Second row: Emily Harper, -?-, Gladys Gould, Hilda Andrews, -?-, Minnie Williams. Front row: the Revd David Howell, Gladys Williams, Florence Allsop, -?-, Madeleine Howell, Agnes Gilbert, Emily Howell, Liza McCabe. *(Ruth Boden)*

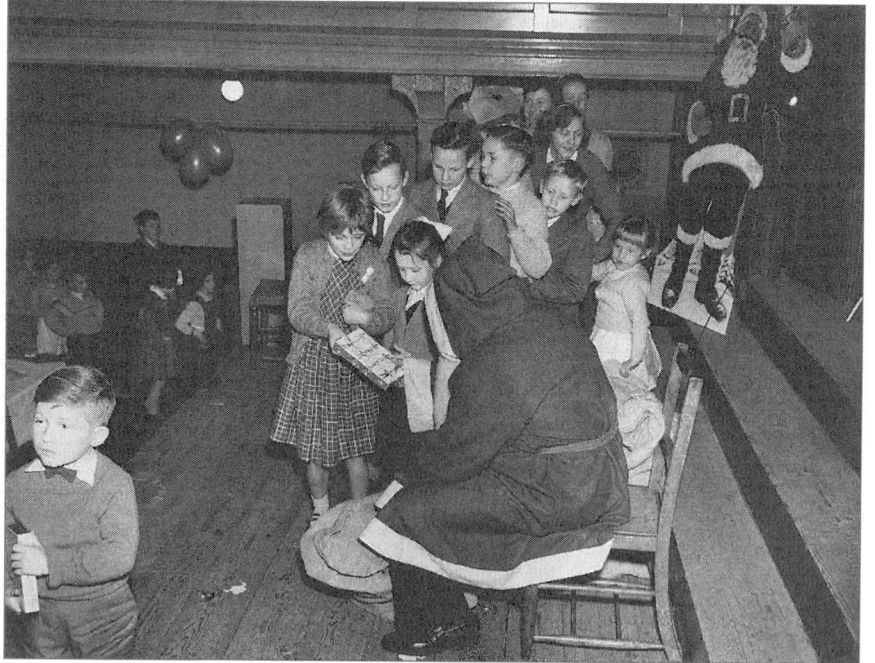

Santa Claus pictured distributing yuletide gifts on behalf of Ratcliffs (GB) Ltd to their employees' children during the firm's annual Christmas party held in West Bromwich Town Hall, *c.* 1961. This firm of metal rollers operated out of two locations, known as No. 1 and No. 2 Works, in the Great Bridge/Golds Hill area. Children receiving gifts are, left to right, William Walker, -?-, Olwyn Dyke, Alan Exall, Kenneth Exall. *(Olwyn Dyke)*

Bagnall Street, Golds Hill, looking towards the canal bridge and the Miners Arms public house (centre), *c.* 1938. On the extreme left are the entrances to St Paul's vicarage and the church hall while further along on the same side is Pikehelve Street. All of the houses on the left, along with the canal, have now gone but those on the right remain today. *(Beryl Wootton)*

Ratcliffs FC line up for a photograph at the Hawthorns before losing 2–1 to Wellington Tube Works FC in the final of the Albion Shield, 1951. Back row, left to right: ? Fisher, -?-, ? Smith, -?-, Horace Budworth, Howard Whale, -?-, Horace Bowen, William Smith, Arthur Curtis. Front row: -?-, Stan Bates, Tom Hackwood, Albert Hickinbottom, Dickie Penn. *(Amy Budworth)*

Hill Top Foundry FC, winners of the Bass Challenge Cup (centre) and West Bromwich Charity Cup, *c*. 1961. Back row, left to right: Albert Perkins, Bernard Cole, Les Tolliday, Billy Andrews. Middle row: Brian Miles, Ted Mason, Ivor Hodgetts, Jim Young, Brian Wilson, Brian Woolhouse. Front row: Tom Bunn, Brian Nunns, Tony Walton, Terry McHale, George Shingleton, Brian Priest, Trevor Perkins. *(Trevor Perkins)*

Hill Top British Legion FC, members of the Warwickshire & West Midland Football Alliance, *c*. 1972. Back row, left to right: Brian Hickman, Ray Bull, Kevin Satchwell, Tony Stokes, Paul Wareham, John Willetts, David Griffiths, Arthur Brown, John Richards. Front row: Malcolm Shinton, Malcolm Evans, Trevor Garman, John Birch, Robert Lloyd, Keith Rollinson. *(Trevor Garman)*

New Street FC, members of the West Bromwich & District Saturday League, 1955/56. Back row, left to right: Fred Millward, George Arnold, Ken Rotten, -?-, Ron Hall. Middle row: Billy Upton, Tom Eden, Jack Bishop, Frank Watts, Harry Bishop, Rex Arnold, Joe Rudge, Ray Whittaker, Geoff Hill, Ron Mottram. Front row: Len Riley, Gerald 'Jetta' Arnold, Ernie Whitehouse, Derek Stokes, Ron 'Nobby' Taylor, Fred Bradley. (Derek Stokes)

Hill Top Amateurs FC, pictured on the King George VI playing fields, c. 1967. Back row, left to right: Alan ?, Jimmy Gittins, David Bishop, Ken Smith, Jimmy Davies, Barry Stokes, John Morris, Terry Askey, Patrick 'Paddy' Malloy. Front row: Mick Plant, Dennis Parks, John Lester, Mel Kent, Ken Price, Brian Bishop. (Mel Kent)

An aerial view of Hill Top in about 1949 showing Hawkes Lane (bottom), Queen Street (left), Castle Street (top) and the main road through Holloway Bank to Wednesbury on the right. In the centre of the picture are the premises of Hill Top Foundry, established by Edward Elwell in 1799. (*Trevor Perkins*)

Customers pictured at the rear of the British Oak, Hawkes Lane, *c*. 1920. Amos Jones, the landlord from 1914 to 1943, was previously at the White Swan, also in Hawkes Lane. He is sitting in the second row, third from the right. Mary Elizabeth Jones is on the left while Tillie Jackson is the lady on the right. Harry Jackson is immediately behind Amos Jones. *(Roma Bannister)*

Hill Top Methodist Church Sunday School anniversary, *c*. 1958. Back row, first, ninth and twelfth from left: Doreen Cowles, Susan Jones, Kath Withers. Middle row: Margaret Kerr, -?-, Linda Fenton, Barbara Williams, -?-, Amy Marsden, Janet Jones, Lynn Shilton, Barbara Marsden, -?-, -?-, Doreen Marsters. Front row, first and sixth: Alice Duncombe, Linda Williams. *(Amy Budworth)*

Amy Howard's confectionery shop at 24 New Street, Hill Top, *c. 1929*. Although the business was registered in William Edgar Howard's name between 1918 and 1934, and in Amy's from 1934 to when the shop closed in 1958, it was she who effectively ran this establishment on a day-to-day basis. Previous shopkeepers at this address had been Mary Ann Earp (1890–94), William Cashmore (1894–1902), Rosana Silk (1902–14) and Thomas Jeavon (1914–18). *(Amy Budworth)*

Below: Shops on the main Wednesbury–West Bromwich road at Hill Top pictured in about 1914. They include, from left to right, Humphrey Lugg – ironmonger, established at 39 Hawkes Lane in 1890, Hill Top post office – taken over by Paul Barton in about 1915, Frederick Clark – cycle agent, Albert John Parish – bootmaker and Josiah & Edward Griffiths – furniture brokers. *(Barry Smith)*

Hill Top, showing from right to left the council school and Humphrey Lugg's new ironmongery premises, *c.* 1930. Hill Top school, which opened in 1911, had its assembly hall and two classrooms destroyed by enemy bombing in 1940. By 1952 both the infants and juniors had been transferred to Hateley Heath school leaving Hill Top solely as a secondary modern. In 1969 it became a comprehensive high school. *(T.J.H. Price)*

The main road from Black Lake to Hill Top where a distant Birmingham Corporation tramcar, en route to Wednesbury, is about to pass the junctions of New Street and Coles Lane, *c.* 1925. After improvements to Holyhead Road and Holloway Bank in the eighteenth and nineteenth centuries, this highway became part of the revised coaching route between London and Holyhead. *(Ken Rock)*

Ye Olde Hill Top Coffee House, 80 Hill Top, *c.* 1965. These refreshment rooms first appeared in trade records in 1886 showing James Thomas Carter as the proprietor. Coincidentally, another Carter, Mary Alice, occupied these premises from 1934 to 1950, with Thomas Wheatley (1904) and Josiah Griffiths (1904–34) residing here in the intervening period. Others were Albert and Winifred Downes (1950–9), George and Annie Morgan (1959–62) and finally, before it closed in 1963, Arthur and Pamela Copson. *(Ken Smith)*

The Hen and Chickens, 90 Hill Top, *c.* 1967. Howard Heath was the licensee at this time. Coach passengers travelling between London and Holyhead in the early nineteenth century would have certainly availed themselves of this inn's facilities, which at that time would have been provided by landlord Joseph Belcher. Elkanah Boyes (1858–78) and Richard Quance (1886–1902) were other early long-serving licensees. *(Andrew Maxam)*

Hill Top looking towards Holloway Bank and St James Church in the distance with one of the many locations of Hill Top post office shown on the left, *c. 1963*. The police station and library situated next to St James's Church were built in 1897/98 on the site of Meyrick House, the home of Joseph Hateley, a solicitor in the early nineteenth century. *(Alan Price)*

George Mason's grocery store at 178 Hill Top pictured just eight years after it opened in 1922. Notice the large number of staff that these shops employed compared with those of today. George Mason's shop near Carters Green had eleven! Standing outside, second and third from the left are brother and sister, Reg and Rene Timms. This branch closed in about 1969. *(Heather Noake)*

Players and supporters of New Street FC pictured at the Fountain Inn, Holloway Bank before their annual dinner, *c. 1955*. Among those at the back: Stan Riley, Harry Howard, Ron Mottram, Geoff Hill, Frank Mottram, Fred Smith, Jack Howard, Ken Rotten, Jack Bishop, Bill Hollyhead. Second row: Len Hopcroft, Fred Bradley, George Starkey, Tom Eden, Lucy Riley. Front row: Ron 'Nobby' Taylor, Derek Stokes, Rose Mottram, Finis Mottram, Joan Upton, Billy Harris. *(Derek Stokes)*

The Fountain Inn, 132 Holloway Bank, when Albert Parsons was the licensee, *c. 1963*. This is the second of two Fountain Inns to have occupied this site, the first dating back to at least 1834 when Charles Wilson was the landlord. The old pub was noted for the longevity of its licensees; George Willetts and his family (1902–30) were the best known. *(T.J.H. Price)*

John Johnson's off-licence at 4 Crookhay Lane, Hill Top, *c.* 1949. These licensed premises, belonging to Darby's Brewery Ltd of Greets Green, had only nine occupants from about 1860 to when it closed on 18 February 1960. The full list is as follows: John Turner (*c.* 1860–82), Mary Ann Turner (1882–1914), George Smith (1914–18), Mark Simpson (1918–22), Charlotte Gould (1922–6), Samuel Green (1926–38), Richard James Thursfield (1938–46), Eleanor and Elena M. Richards (1947), John Johnson (1 July 1948–18 February 1960). *(Andrew Maxam)*

Below: The Three Horseshoes, 86 Witton Lane, Hill Top, 26 May 1965. Sidney Frederick Williams was the licensee at this time. For twenty-eight years from 1866 to 1894 the licence for this pub was held by two members of the Davis family, John (1866–70) and Mary (1870–94). In more recent times Rebecca Laight was here for almost fourteen years between 4 July 1957 and 9 March 1961. Almost opposite at 91 Witton Lane and in front of Rydding Square was, until it was demolished in about 1936, the Golden Lion public house. The last two licensees of this old hostelry were the Dugmores. Joseph (1914–30) was succeeded by his wife Emily Clare (1930–6). *(Andrew Maxam)*

The Millfield Inn, Rydding Lane, West Bromwich, 26 March 1962, when James Reginald Guest was the licensee. The first landlord of this pub when it opened in 1938 was Arthur Edwin Cole who had previously been licensee at the Old Crown in Harvills Hawthorn. Several years ago The Millfield became known as Cagney's & Lacy's but was later changed again to its present title The Old Mill. *(T.J.H. Price)*

The bar of The Millfield Inn, Rydding Lane, where staff, friends and relatives of the licensee, Arthur Edwin Cole, pose for a photograph, *c.* 1950. Back row, left to right: ? Parkes, ? Goldie, -?-, Hilda Trusslove, Vinny Russell, Arthur Cole, Harry Russell, Lily Lawley, Arthur Hanley. Front row: ? Parkes, ? Goldie, Vera Baker, ? Bell, Rachel Cole, Arthur Cole Jnr, Arthur Edwin Cole, Lily Cole, Dolly Royce, ? Hanley. *(Arthur Cole)*

Chapter Five
Great Barr, Lyndon
& Tantany

Assembled colliers, with their new banner, prepare to take part in the annual Hamstead Colliery Miners' Gala, June 1956. Those in the picture include Alf Seabright, Jimmy Clapperton, Billy Parker, Les Colstan, Ted Morgan, Ewan Wyld, Dennis Evans, Frank Ward, Reg Hassell, Eddie Kindley, Jock Welsh, Stan Priest, Alan Smith, Sam Henderson, Ted Leatherland, Gwyn Probyn, Fred Probyn, Joe Hill, Sam Whitehouse, Joe Leatherland, Alan Ward, Billy Love, Reg Talbot, Bert Wright, Billy Leatherland, Charlie Cross, Jack Rowley. *(Hamstead Social Club)*

A view of the old Newton Road, Great Barr, looking towards Ray Hall Lane in the distance, 8 March 1964. A West Bromwich Corporation Metro-Cammell Daimler CVG6/30 bus, on the No. 6 Hamstead–Dartmouth Square service, is seen passing the construction of a new dual carriageway on the right. *(David Wilson)*

The Malt Shovel, Newton Road, March 1961. Alexander Gilbert was the licensee at the time. This building replaced a previous inn of the same name in about 1935. The first landlord of the premises above was Henry Whitehouse who remained here for fifteen years until Isaac Bradley took over in 1950. Since then pub has been structurally altered internally several times, together with an enlargement of the adjacent car park. *(Sidney Darby & Son Ltd)*

Allen Memorial Dramatic Society's production of two one-act plays entitled *And Now – The Journey* and *Ladies-In-Waiting*, 23 October 1948. Back row, left to right: Walter Spears, Tim Plowman, Fred Searle, Harold Cooper, Sid Edwards, T.A. Shakespeare, the Revd John Dilwyn Williams, -?-. Front row: Ethel Leedham, Irene Turner, ? Aspbury, Betty Edwards, Iris Edge, Hilda Searle, Fay Lillicrap, Kay Cook, Olive Edwards, Audrey Shakespeare. *(Carol Leedham)*

The Scott Arms, corner of Newton Road and Walsall Road Great Barr, *c.* 1960. Harry Worthington was the licensee at the time. This old coaching inn dating from 1786 was demolished in 1966 in preparation for the planned improvements in road layout which were to take place before the construction of the M5/M6 interchange. *(Andrew Maxam)*

An interior view of the new and luxurious Scott Arms public house just before its official opening on 15 August 1968. The lounge area looks quite different to this now, having recently been subject to a major refurbishment. The pub has proven to be popular with patrons of the adjacent Scott Arms Shopping Centre which was built at the same time as these premises. *(Andrew Maxam)*

Birmingham Road, Great Barr, *c.* 1960. This view looks towards Cross Lane and the Roman Catholic Church of the Holy Name, erected in 1938. The Walsall & District Co-operative Society building on the left is presently occupied by Machine Mart Ltd, while the adjacent row of shops now has a service road in front of them. *(Anthony Page)*

Walsall Road, Great Barr, looking towards Jayshaw Avenue on the left and the Scott Arms public house up ahead, *c.* 1940. Towering above the surrounding buildings at the junction of Birmingham Road and Queslett Road is the Beacon Cinema which was opened in 1938 by Cllr Clifford Rowley, Chairman of the Highways Committee, Aldridge District Council. The architect was R. Satchwell LRIBA. *(Anthony Page)*

The Beacon Cinema, Scott Arms, opened on Monday 7 March 1938 with the film *Oh, Mr. Porter!* starring Will Hay, Moore Marriott and Graham Moffatt. The cinema, pictured here in about 1973, had a seating capacity of 1,200 and was made entirely in reinforced concrete, except for the steel roof trusses. The final films shown were *The Nympho* and *Erotic Three* when it closed on 16 December 1972. Demolition followed in June 1976. In the foreground are Simon Cotter (left) and Kevin Cotter. *(Maurice Cotter)*

The Beacon public house, Birmingham Road, Great Barr, *c.* 1965. Roy Compton was the landlord at this time. This was another modern replacement for an older nineteenth-century building which from 1905 to 1925, had John Pritchard as its longest-serving licensee. The premises above became a Harvester restaurant in 1998 with separate hotel facilities, known as Holiday Inn Express, having been built at the rear. *(Andrew Maxam)*

Hamstead Road, with Tanhouse Avenue on the right, April 1966. A West Bromwich Corporation Metro-Cammell Weymann-bodied Daimler CVG6 bus on the No. 6 route is travelling to its terminus in Green Lane before returning to the Scott Arms. Above the skyline in the background is Hamstead Colliery which ceased operation 1965. *(Graham Harper)*

Queen Elizabeth II coronation celebrations in Spouthouse Lane, Great Barr, 2 June 1953. Left group: Marjorie Stokes, Blanche Stokes, Isobel Stokes, Edie Brown, Ethel Bisp, Anne McCann, Doris Phillips, Pat Bisp. Centre group: Louise Taylor, Joyce Taylor, Janet Turley, Pat Harvey, Margaret Stevens. Right group: Horace Stevens, Blanche Stevens, Marjorie Sanderson, Rosalind Taylor, Doreen Taylor, Flora Thomas, Dennis Taylor, Terry Morris. *(Doreen Young)*

Railway Terrace, Hamstead Village, *c.* 1930. These business premises make an interesting comparison with those of today. Left to right in 1930: -?-, -?-, greengrocery shop, Keasey's newsagents, bakery/shop, Wright's Shoes, Bailey's confectionery, -?-, hairdresser/post office. Left to right in 2006: Nationwide, Domani nail and tanning salon, Images hairstylists, Hamstead Law Practice, Blue Moon Café, Flowers 'R' Us florist, Sea Garden Chinese takeaway, Garden Two Chinese & Pizza, post office. *(Anthony Page)*

The Red Admiral, 52 Gorse Farm Road, Great Barr, *c.* 1965. John Frank Watson was the licensee here from 6 July 1961 to 23 July 1970. The premises opened on 6 March 1959 under the management of Jack Robinson. Since Mitchells & Butlers' original ownership there have been four others to date: Bass Ltd, Mitchells & Butlers Taverns Ltd, Bass Leisure Retail and the Unique Pub Co. Ltd. *(Andrew Maxam)*

Sponsored entrants in the Sandwell Area Health Authority's 'Healthy Sandwell 2000 Bike Ride' pictured waiting for the starting pistol on the out-patients car park of Sandwell General Hospital in Little Lane. Cyclists in the foreground from Cronehills Health Centre are Jill and Steve Cartwright (left, on the tandem) and Beryl Price (number 69). *(T.J.H. Price)*

The Jolly Nailor public house, Lyndon, 7 July 1968. Harry Rose was the landlord when this picture was taken but even his eight-year service could not match that of John Cotterell who served from 1850 to 1878 and Alfred Griffin from 1906 to 1930. The property on the left, occupied by Lyndon Laundry Ltd who were established here in 1914, was demolished in 2005. *(Alan Price)*

The Five Ways Inn (The Fourpenny shop), 58 Seager Street, annual darts team dinner, *c.* 1948. Seated around the left table, clockwise: Frank Moore, Joe Harris, Jimmy Simpkins, Reg Box, Jack Poulton. Standing at the back: Sam Woodfield, Bert Willetts (licensee 1938–58), Jack Brookes. Standing between the tables: -?-, Joan Willetts, Alice Willetts. Right table, front right: Jack Thompson. Under the picture frame, second from the right: Tom Shelton. *(Tom Shelton)*

A mammoth outing from the Five Ways Inn pictured at the junction of Taylors Lane and St Clements Lane, *c.* 1947. It was organised by the licensee Bert Willetts who is standing beneath the Belisha beacon on the left. Jack Brookes is fourth from left, back row. Frank Moore is third from right of the beacon. Joseph Shelton is first on the left, front row. Others in the crowd are Walter Powell, Arthur Cresswell, Ethel Walker, Elizabeth Sedgley, Sid Sedgley and Sam Box. *(Tom Shelton)*

The Theatre Royal, Walsall Street, from a painting by local artist Geoffrey Southall, *c.* 1964. Charles Udall, a beer house keeper of the adjoining Royal Exchange, erected this building in 1850; it was originally known as Udall's Free and Easy. On 29 September 1879, twenty-six years after becoming a licensed concert hall, it was given the new name of the Theatre Royal. Eventually in June 1940 it was closed and during the building's final years was used for furniture storage by Hill & Long Ltd. *(Betty Law)*

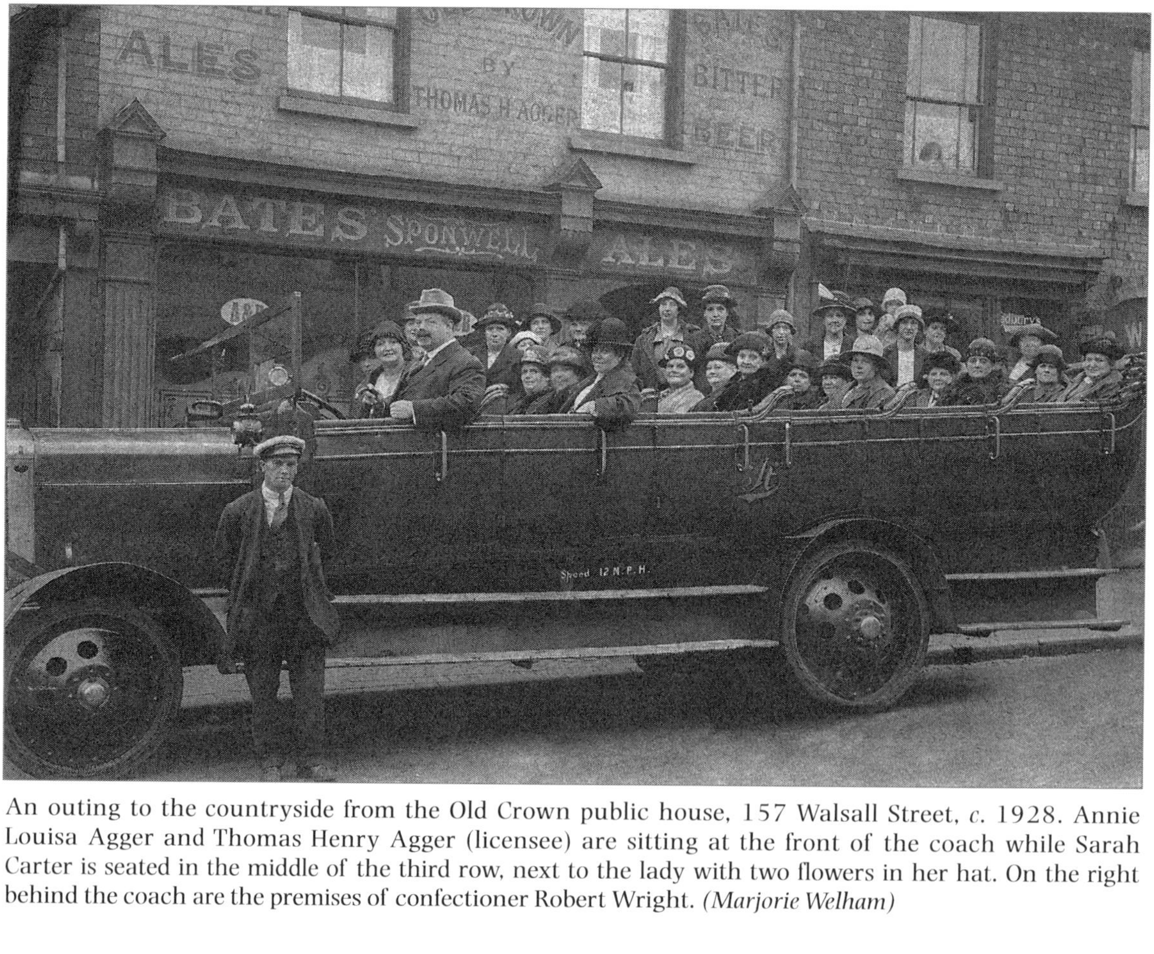

An outing to the countryside from the Old Crown public house, 157 Walsall Street, *c.* 1928. Annie Louisa Agger and Thomas Henry Agger (licensee) are sitting at the front of the coach while Sarah Carter is seated in the middle of the third row, next to the lady with two flowers in her hat. On the right behind the coach are the premises of confectioner Robert Wright. *(Marjorie Welham)*

Corner shops in Sandwell Road at the junction with Beale Street, 1940. William and Caroline Pitt's confectionery shop is on the left, which had a change of ownership in 1950 when John and Keziah Warner took over. On the right are James Birch's greengrocery premises, taken over by John and Hilda Griffiths in 1945. The final owners from 1949 to 1967 were Alfred and Emily Grice. Note the bicycle tyre on the shop's roof. *(T.J.H. Price)*

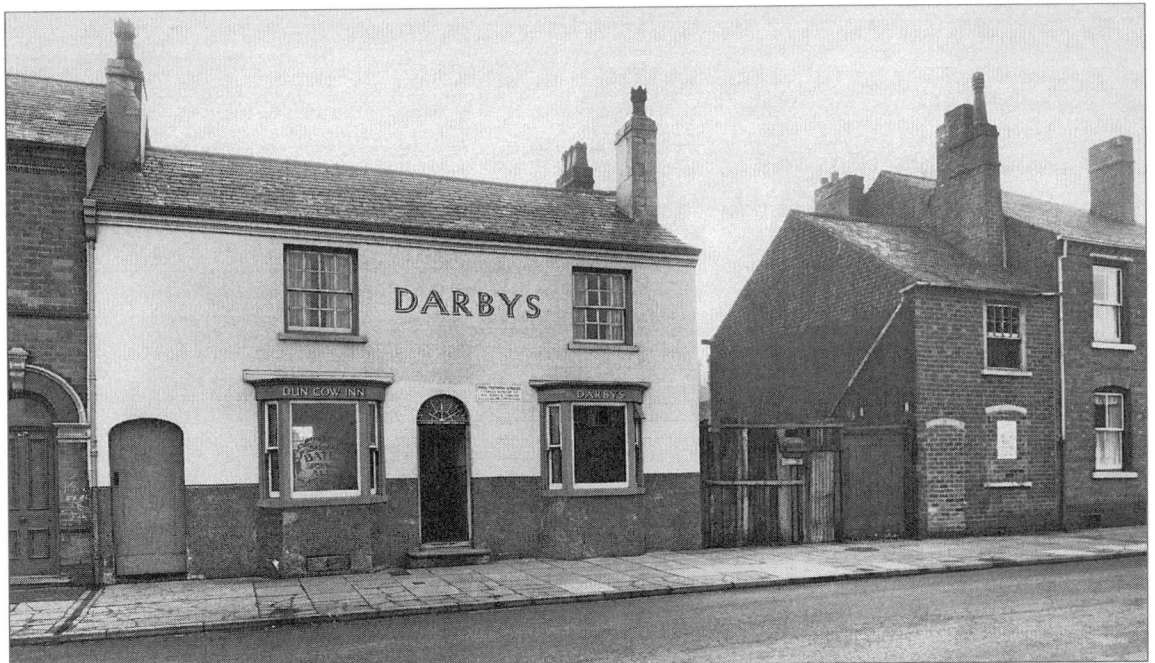

The Dun Cow, 173 Sandwell Road, 18 February 1960. Paul Thomas O'Neill was the landlord. The first recorded licensee was Maria Stevens who managed this beer house between 1878 and 1886. She was succeeded by one Joseph Chinn who went on to occupy these premises for a record twelve years; no doubt he was an ancestor of BBC radio presenter and historian Dr Carl Chinn. The pub closed on 28 May 1969. *(Andrew Maxam)*

Scott Street looking towards Lyndon in the distance, 1961. This stretch of roadway has since been replaced by a dual carriageway now called All Saints Way. The West Bromwich Corporation Willowbrook-bodied Daimler CVG6/30 bus is operating on the No. 8 Stone Cross–Dartmouth Square route. *(David Wilson)*

The Plumbers Arms, 113 Hargate Lane, March 1961. Kenneth George Toussaint was the licensee at the time. These premises date back to at least 1845 when *Kelly's Trade Directory* shows landlord John Watson living here. When it closed on 24 July 1977 the licence was transferred to the China Clipper, which in November 1996 changed its name to the Hargate Arms. *(Sidney Darby & Son Ltd)*

Tavern Rovers FC,
c. 1957/58. Back row,
left to right: Harry
Grainger, Ray Evans,
Cecil Flanagan, Frank
Griffiths, Eric Lloyd,
Peter Wilkes, Ernie
Holmes, Harry Evans.
Front row: Tom Harris,
Cliff Lloyd, Jim Hinton,
Arthur Cooper, Les
Pace. *(Ernie Holmes)*

VE Day party at the rear of Emmies pawnshop, 9 Hargate Lane, 8 May 1945. Back row, left to right:
John Woodfield, Geoff Williams, Malcolm Meades, Alan Frost, Ken Baggott, Robin Corbett, -?-, Jean
Edwards, Heather Payton, Emma Baggott, Pat Harris, -?-, ? Munslow, Irene Munslow, Sam Edwards.
Third row: June Knight, Brian Henley, Maureen Timms, Avril Payton, Harry Burns, Judy Corbett,
Eric Noake, Kathleen Harris, ? Munslow, Eileen Bunch, Jean Williams. Second row: Billy Holder, Brian
Williams, Roy Edwards, Ernest Rowley, David Timms. Front row: -?-, Bobby Burns, -?-, Sheila Collins,
Joan Collins, Albert Walker, Christine Frost. *(Sheila Haynes)*

West Bromwich swimming club, prize distribution evening, *c.* 1976. The club was based at the Sons of Rest building in Dagger Lane. Back row, left to right: -?-, Richard Hipkiss, Alan Brookes, Michael Donald. Front row: ? Nock, Terry Parker, Billie Newbould, Kay Parker, Chris Cooper, Charles Martin (President), Terry Newbould, Chris Padbury, Ian Denning, David Newbould. *(Graham Denning)*

Dagger Lane, looking from Salters Lane on the right, *c.* 1930. Dagger Hall, owned in 1667 by William Turton of the Oak House, was located at this junction until its demolition between July 1894 and February 1895. The avenue of trees also pictured on the right were transferred here from the Hill House estate when the roadway was widened in the late nineteenth century. *(T.J.H. Price)*

The Leopard, 60 Church Vale, March 1961. Although the licensee's name over the door is shown as Edwin Henry Reynolds, he was better known as Harry. This was to be his last public house (1959–64) before moving to an off-licence in Marsh Lane. Earlier he had managed the Cricketers Arms (1936–43), the Bush Inn (1943–51) and the Victoria Inn (1951–9). Leopard landlords from the past include William Reeves (1870–82) and John Bates who was in charge for twenty-four years from 1914 to 1938. The Leopard finally ceased trading on 15 August 1965 with Ronald Rennie on record as the last licensee. On 22 October 1970 new licensed premises, the Four in Hand, opened on the corner of Tenscore Street and Parsonage Street as a replacement for The Leopard and the nearby Ring of Bells. However, the Four in Hand also closed in about 1995 with the site now occupied by a McDonald's restaurant. *(Sidney Darby & Son Ltd)*

Dartmouth Garage, Church Vale, *c.* 1930, the second with this name to be opened by the three Hadlington brothers who are probably the gentlemen pictured above. Their main depot was at 386 High Street but by 1976 the business had been acquired by Charles Clarke Ltd for £300,000. These High Street premises eventually closed altogether in 2005, by which time it was known as Hartwell Charles Clarke Ltd. *(T.J.H. Price)*

The Lodge Theatre Society's production of *The Dancing Years* at the Gayton Road Community Centre in 1975. Formed in about 1956, this theatrical group survived for forty years before disbanding in 1996. From left to right: Miriam Evans, Alan Keeling, Arthur Harris, Cyril Randle, Marjorie Sever, Jim Laing, Eileen Povey, Jack Pardoe, Roma Holloway, Maureen Maydew, Terry Cartwright (producer). *(Alan Keeling)*

The Crown & Cushion, Lloyd Street, with Seager Street on the left, pictured in March 1961 during licensee Ivy Selina Elbro's five-month occupancy. The pub was originally owned by Holders Brewery before being taken over by Mitchells & Butlers Ltd in 1919. Stanley Davies, ex-West Bromwich Albion and Wales international football player, was landlord here between 1930 and 1934. *(Sidney Darby & Son Ltd)*

VE Day street party held for residents of Alton Grove and Stanley Road, 8 May 1945. Around the table from top to bottom, left: Elsie Allsopp, -?-, -?-, -?-, Emily Yates, Ethel Randle, Walter Randle; top to bottom right: Hilda Cooper, -?-, -?-, -?-, -?-, Lily Neary, Peter Pool. Standing, right: Phyliss Sperring (holding Susan Gooding). *(Susan Nock)*

Chapter Six

Charlemont, Friar Park, Stone Cross & Yew Tree

A residents' and shopkeepers' outing from the Stone Cross area to the Cardingmill Valley, Shropshire, *c.* 1954. Back row, left to right: Roy Franks, Paddy McMarn, Fred Evans. Seventh row: Percy Baker, ? Johnson, Jack Worthington. Sixth row: Allan Denning, Jack Smith, Bill Knight. Fifth row: Stan Reading, Len Baker, ? Bicknall, ? Reading, Elsie Deakin, -?-, ? Evans, Alf Wilkes, ? Evans. Fourth row: Margaret Denning, Lucy Minchle, ? Evans, Geoff Franks. Third row: ? Day, Nellie Freeman, Alan Baker, Christine Freeman, Cynthia Wilkes, Vida Wilkes, Dora Denning, Kath Minchle, Kath Worthington. Second row: Elsie Reynolds, ? Day, Neil Franks, Ann Worthington, Robert Franks, Michael Franks, Winnie Franks. Front row: Beverley Wilkes, Diana Deakin, Zarener Jones. *(Graham Denning)*

The grounds of Heath Lane Cemetery where residents of Walsall Road held a VE party on 8 May 1945 to celebrate the end of the Second World War. Back row, first from right: Marjorie Jepson (holding Tony Stokes) with George Jepson to her right. Also pictured is Rebecca Aston while Pauline Jepson and Brenda Collins are sixth and seventh from the right respectively. *(Olive Stokes)*

Hollyhedge Road, Charlemont, with Pennyhill Lane on the right, *c.* 1935. This photograph was taken before the erection of the re-sited Crown & Anchor public house which from 1957 would occupy the area where the bushes are on the right. One of the earliest council estates in West Bromwich was built in this area of Charlemont in the 1920s. *(T.J.H. Price)*

The Crown & Anchor, better known as 'The Jinglers', 73 Hollyhedge Road, when Thomas Alfred Broomhall was the licensee, *c.* 1965. The nickname refers to a previous landlord of the old premises at No. 39, Teddy Carpenter (licensee 1914–34), who had a habit of 'jingling' coins in the pocket of an apron he wore when on duty. The new Crown & Anchor (above) opened on 3 October 1957. *(Andrew Maxam)*

Charlemont Star FC, members of the West Bromwich Sunday League, 1966/67. Back row, left to right: Ken Law, Noel Jones, Gordon Lee, Alan ?, Tony Rzepkowski, Keith Rzepkowski, Garth Thomas (secretary/manager). Front row: George Bunch, Bob Langford, Arthur Brown, Fred Smith, Sam Plant. *(Garth Thomas)*

Charlemont Boxing Club, based at the local secondary modern school in Hollyhedge Road, *c.* 1955. Back row, left to right: -?-, John Adams, Ron Hayes, Norris Webster, -?-, Jule Stockley. Front row: Roy Farmer. Harry Dent, -?-, Jimmy Badhams, -?-, Garth Thomas. *(Garth Thomas)*

Children from the Charlemont and Stone Cross areas celebrating the coronation of Queen Elizabeth II, 2 June 1953. Back row, left to right: Graham Denning, Tony Franks, ? Stevens, Len Baker, Roy Lester. Third row: Ruth Wheatley, Diana Deakin, ? Wilkes, -?-, ? Morton, ? Birks, Alan Baker, Cynthia Wilkes, -?-. Second row: Stephen Jones, -?-, Roy Franks, -?-, Neil Franks, John Morris, Malcolm Franks, ? Shaw, Brian Morton, Bobby Jones. Front row: -?-, Penny Farr, ? Earpe, Robert Reynolds, Robert Franks, Beverley Wilkes, Jennifer Fenton, -?-, Pat Freeman, Gina Evans, Zarener Jones. *(Graham Denning)*

The Mill public house, at the corner of Beaconview Road and Wyndmill Crescent, Charlemont Farm Estate, *c.* 1967. Thomas Clarence Egginton was granted a full licence for these premises on 12 January 1967 and remained here until he was succeeded by Tom Edwards on 6 January 1972. There have been ten licensees since, the latest and record holder from 2 August 2000 being Joseph John Partridge. *(Andrew Maxam)*

Mill Rovers FC, District 4 cup winners and Division 4 runners-up to Jensen Motors in the West Bromwich Sunday League, 1973/74. One of their more unusual pre-season friendly matches around this period was against the British Army in Berlin. Back row, left to right: B. Nutting, -?-, T. Timmins, Philip Corbett, -?-, -?-. Front row: J. Skitt, -?-, B. Timmins, Ronnie 'Rocky' Wallett, Tommy Felton, Colin Barnfield. *(Val Southall)*

Bustleholme Lane, Charlemont at the junction of Jervoise Lane (left), *c.* 1932. Its continuation directly ahead provided access to Bustleholme Mill, thought originally to have belonged to William Comberford, Lord of Wednesbury Manor, who sold the property to Walter Stanley, Lord of West Bromwich, in 1595. What remained of the mill was demolished in 1971. *(T.J.H. Price)*

Bustleholme Lane looking south towards Jervoise Lane showing houses numbered 40 to 56, from left to right, between the telegraph poles, *c.* 1932. This view looks much the same today, with only a change in the street lighting and a few external home improvements having taken place in the intervening years. *(T.J.H. Price)*

Crowds lining the pavement in Walsall Road, Stone Cross, near the junction with Marsh Lane waiting to catch a glimpse of Queen Elizabeth II as she passes by during her Silver Jubilee tour of 1977. The highlight of the Queen's official visit to West Bromwich was her arrival at the town's most famous building, the Oak House. *(Graham Denning)*

The premises of Allan Denning, butcher, and Walter Charles Deakin, chemist, at 92 and 94 Walsall Road, Stone Cross, June 1953. Allan Denning Snr established his butcher's business at 47–9 All Saints Street in 1906, and later acquired the shop (seen here) in 1934. In 1952 Allan Denning Jnr took over the business which afterwards was continued by his son Graham until his retirement in 2001. W.C. Deakin's chemist shop opened here in 1949. *(Graham Denning)*

Hartland Road (left) at the junction of Sheldon Road (right), *c.* 1932. The flower bed and rockery in the foreground, belonged to Edith and Stanley Aulton at No. 34 Hartland Road. They won first prize in the West Bromwich Council gardens competition, which in those days was an annual event. *(Lawrence Aulton)*

The Good Cheer Cellars off-licence, also known as the Pheasant Stores, 32 Marsh Lane, Stone Cross, *c.* 1962. Ray Malcolm Turley was the licence holder between 1961 and 1964 while Geoffrey Biddle was the longest-serving tenant of these ex-Darby's premises from 1972 to 1992. Harry Reynolds was also a licensee here for almost six years until his retirement from the trade on 23 October 1969. *(Andrew Maxam)*

Moorlands Church, Hall Green Road, Sunday School anniversary, *c. 1950*. Back row, left to right: Eddie Fisher, Alan Jewkes, -?-, -?-, Norma Parkes, Sandra Farnell, Margaret Jones, Robert Powell, -?-, -?-, Barry Wharton. Among the third row: Audrey Kennerley, Roderick Jennings, Margaret Gilbert, Dyllis Tyack, David Spiers, Dorothy Benning. Second row: Margaret Glendenning, John Peplow, David Peplow, Wendy Addison, -?-, Pam Whitehouse, -?-, Margaret Sheldon, -?-, Christine Irish, -?-, Sylvia Addison. Front row: Heather Jones, Wendy Cooper, Janet Allen, Stephanie Bridge, Norma Gould. In 1959 this mission church was relocated to Hydes Road. *(Doreen Davies)*

Members of the Moorlands Church youth club, 1951/52. Back row, left to right: Frank Davies, Florence Cooper, Irene Bunn, Jean Moore, -?-, -?-, Margaret Wilkins, Gladys Ellis, Norma Gould, Derek Davies, Ron Bullock. Among the middle row: Jenny Spiers, Margaret Smith, Arthur Gould, Geoffrey Williams, Gordon Yates, Raymond Bissell. Front row: Mary Moore, Margaret Glendenning, Valerie Yates, Doreen Davies (with Ken Davies), Dorothy Benning, Mary Haffner, Irene Gould, Eddie Fisher. *(Doreen Davies)*

The men's annual supper at Moorlands Church, *c*. 1963. Back row, standing left to right: Kenneth Cartwright, John Winchurch, Raymond Bissell, Ben Winchurch, Bert Jones, Frank Davies, Gerald Hughes, Horace Jones, David Irish, William Webb, Hubert Bayley, Anne ? , Albert Partridge, Alf Benning, Michael Kennett, Jim Canavan, David Pallett, Alan Lloyd, Howard Bayley, Kenneth Davies, Arthur Wharton, William Cooper. Front table: -?-, -?-, -?-, May Webb, Joyce Berrow, ? Berrow, Doreen Davies, Mary Partridge, Irene Davies. Left corner: Dennis Onions. *(Doreen Davies)*

The 9th West Bromwich Company Boys' Brigade football team, based at Moorlands Church, Hydes Road, February 1967. Back row, left to right: Alan Davies, Jim Canavan, David Holden, David Pallett, Peter Holloway. Front row: Ken Davies, Roy Statham, Alan Lloyd, John Wilkinson, John Bissell, David Jordan. *(Doreen Davies)*

Stone Cross cinema (formerly the Clifton) partially obscured by a West Bromwich Corporation bus in Hall Green Road, 1963. This cinema was opened by actress Valerie Hobson on Saturday 16 July 1938 with the film *Whoopee!*, starring Eddie Cantor. The last film to be shown here before it was completely taken over by bingo in 1964 was *Doctor No*, starring Sean Connery. It remained a bingo hall until closure in 2003; demolition followed in September 2005. *(Graham Harper)*

Stone Cross FC, winners of the Warwickshire & West Midland Alliance Premier League and the Birmingham Senior Cup, *c.* 1968. Back row, left to right: Harry Williams, John Ainge, John Richards, Fred Furnival, Jimmy Carter, Cliff Hedges, Derek Hopkins, Fred Woodcock. Front row: Trevor Roberts, Bobby Hadley, Philip Goode, Trevor Garman, Stan Whitehouse, Arthur Brown. *(Trevor Garman)*

The Sandhills Garage, Walsall Road, Stone Cross, June 1969. This garage and adjoining petrol station were situated next to a large excavation originally known as Bustleholme Sandbeds owned by Frederick C. Lowe Ltd, sand merchants. They sold the land to Mr R. Nutter of Oldbury in 1951 who, three years later disposed of it to the Midland Motor Cylinder Co. Over the next twenty to thirty years extractions of sand and gravel gradually ceased and it was eventually filled in with foundry waste. Houses were built on the site in 1986. *(Alan Price)*

Walsall Road between Stone Cross and the Navigation canal bridge, *c.* 1968. A West Bromwich Corporation Metro-Cammell Daimler CVG6 bus can be seen operating on the short working No. 2T route between Yew Tree Estate and Princes End, Tipton. Beyond the bungalows and petrol station on the right are the present-day locations of Burghley Drive and Millersdale Drive. *(John Whitehouse)*

Walsall Road, Friar Park, where a West Bromwich Willowbrook-bodied sixty-seat Daimler CVG6 bus has just passed over Bescot marshalling yard's railway bridge on the No. 54 Walsall–West Bromwich route, 13 April 1964. On the left are the factory premises of William Mills Ltd, aluminium founders. *(David Wilson)*

Queen Elizabeth II coronation party in Manor Road, Friar Park, 2 June 1953. Among the group, from left to right: Beryl Gibbard, Phoebe Powell, Cissie Beard, Brian Rogers, Hannah Fletcher, John Lane, Brian Beard, Tom Poulton, Christine Poulton, Rhoda Latham, Barry Hughes, Olive Latham, Barbara Bingham, Margaret Long, Doris Bingham, Lily Long, Iris Morton, Mavis Bingham, Mark Hall, Cliff Simcox, Christine Simcox, Lottie Morton, Ann Fletcher, Ernie Rogers, Harold Long, Reg Hughes, Billy Poulton. *(Barbara Perkins)*

Dorset Road, Friar Park, VJ Day celebrations, August 1945. The rear group includes Tony Blackburn, George Leach, Dorothy Wood, Marge Cashmore, Gwen Groom, Betty Cheese, Pearl Ford, Margaret Cook, Gladys Rolls, Kathy Edwards, Beryl Cheese, Marylin Cook, Harry Gaskill. Second row: Brian Elsmore, Roy Elsmore, -?-, Maurice Bailey, Florence Bunn, -?-, -?-, Winnie Groom, ? Adams, Janet Cheese, Edna Cheese, ? Cook. Front row: Teddy Bevin, Ken Russell, Roy Gaskill, Hazel Russell, and eighth from the left, Tom Broomhall. *(Joan Haycock)*

Walsall Road, Friar Park, looking towards a tree-obscured Navigation Inn, Thursday 10 April 1941. This residential area, adjacent to the Bescot railway marshalling yards, shows damage resulting from enemy bombing during the Second World War with the scene also showing the disruption caused to the sewerage system and water supply. *(South Staffs Water)*

Above: A scene of devastation in Roberts Road, Friar Park, following the explosion of a lorry carrying a mixed load of steel and chemicals which had parked nearby on waste ground at 11.00am on Tuesday 6 February 1962. The vehicle had been transporting twelve glass carboys of hydrogen peroxide and seventy-two containers of methyl ethyl ketone from Warrington to the Midlands along the A4031 Walsall Road. *Below:* The same view from the air showing the adjacent Walsall Road near to the Navigation Inn from where the lorry driver John Walker made an emergency telephone call for help after his vehicle had caught fire. *(Harvey Birch)*

Roberts Road, Friar Park, 6 February 1962. Here we see one of the most severely damaged houses which had to be demolished by West Bromwich Corporation, along with five others. A further thirty-six council houses were badly damaged with another 136 only moderately. Thirty-two people were injured – twenty-eight adults and four children – when debris from the lorry and its load was scattered over a radius of 220 yards. The Albion lorry owners were Jack's Motors Ltd of Blackburn, Lancashire. *(Harvey Birch)*

Yew Tree Methodist Church Sunday School anniversary parade entering Brindle Road from Plane Tree Road, Yew Tree Estate, *c.* 1984. At the rear, right: Adele Boddice. Middle group: Ian Wickett, ? Smith, Sarah ?, ? Meek (mostly hidden). Surrounding the banner, from left to right: -?-, Ann Jukes, Keith Brookes, Robert Jukes, Elizabeth ?, -?-. *(Harry Collins)*

The original premises of the Yew Tree Social Club, Brackendale Drive, showing the toilet block (left) and the converted workmen's hut (right), *c.* 1959. Between 1959 and 1968 the committee obtained successive loans of £7,000, £15,000 and £89,000 from Ansells Brewery Ltd in order to rebuild and develop what was to become arguably the finest social club in the Midlands. So successful was this enterprise that all of these loans were easily repaid ahead of time. *(Joe Hall)*

The 10th West Bromwich Company Boys' Brigade, based at Yew Tree Methodist Church. They are pictured in Old Meeting Street while taking part in the town's carnival, *c.* 1968. From left to right: John Bunyard, Tony Gibbard (big drum), Susan Tay, Janet Fellows (tambourine), Richard Mayhew (front right), Raymond Pearce. *(Harry Collins)*

The new and purpose-built Yew Tree Social and Labour Club in Brackendale Drive pictured at the time of its opening, Christmas 1960. The club's original location was a workman's hut which local residents had purchased from the estate builders, Wimpey, for £50 in October 1957. Two years later a loan of £7,000 was obtained from Ansells Brewery Ltd for construction of the building shown here. The club has been extended on two occasions since. *(Joe Hall)*

A tranquil scene in 1969 on the Tame Valley Canal, adjacent to Yew Tree Estate, where local resident Paul Williams appears to be going flat out to catch 'tiddlers' in his submerged net. Standing to his left are Susan Williams and Alf Williams. Birchfield Way provides access to this stretch of the canal, which continues past the rooftops of Bermuda Mansions in the distance. *(Janet Williams)*

Food being prepared for the Women's Fellowship supper held at Yew Tree Methodist Church Hall, Redwood Road, *c.* 1970. The church, which opened on 25 November 1967, eventually closed in 1995 owing to a combination of declining membership and vandalism. From left to right: Clara Whitehouse, Iris Cox, -?-, Gladys Taylor, -?-, Annie Jackson, Celia Edey, Gwen Withers, Ada Dyke, Agnes Collins. *(Harry Collins)*

Cleaning ladies at Yew Tree Social Club, Brackendale Drive say farewell to Ivy Withers on the occasion of her retirement in December 1981 after twenty-one years' service. The club, established in 1957, has undergone three major expansions since its formation which included new concert and snooker rooms. From left to right: Frances Whitehouse, Margaret Gilbert, Barbara Jukes, Evelyn Dunn, Pat Moore, Beryl Wootton, Florence Cross. Front: Ivy Withers. *(Beryl Wootton)*

Chapter Seven

Schooldays

A marvellous picture of the old English tradition of dancing around the maypole, being displayed here by pupils of All Saints' Church of England Infants and Junior School, *c.* 1958. This rarely photographed event is taking place on the vicarage lawn which is overlooked by All Saints' Church in the background.
(Vera Horton)

All Saints' School FC, 1956/57, with sportsmaster Norman Riley standing behind the team. Back row, left to right: Malcolm Wright, Brian Bates, Graham Turner, -?-, Philip Bird, Michael Leadbeater, David Philpot, Robert Kemp. Front row: John Lester, Richard Cohen, Malcolm Bunch, Robert Marsh, Richard Harman. *(Pat Darby)*

All Saints' School FC, 1959/60. Back row, left to right: Geoff Williams (sportsmaster), Ken Jones, Tony 'Tonka' Walton, Frank Garrett (headmaster). Middle row: -?-, Royston Bunn, Keith Rushton, -?-, Stanley Stephenson, Tony Lake. Front row: Barry Smith, Fred Lowe, David Lees, John Smallman, Graham Turner. *(Graham Turner)*

All Saints' School FC, 1960/61. Back row, left to right: Frank Garrett (headmaster), Geoff Williams (sportsmaster). Middle row: Sidney Tolley, Tony Lake, Ken Green, Fred Lowe, Robin Dawes, David Hill, Clive Basford, Terry Bates. Front row: John Smallman, John Lester, Graham Turner, John Holmes, Mick Jones. Clive Basford went on to become a renowned world champion hairstylist, a title he won in Rotterdam in 1980. He currently has a salon at 381 High Street. *(Graham Turner)*

An infants class at All Saints' Church of England School, Christmas, *c.* 1955. Extreme left: Christine Turner. Around the first table, left to right: Kathleen ?, Keith Lake, Jennifer Morris, Ann Law (standing), Lesley Bradley, -?-, Geoffrey Love, Sidney Oakley (on floor). Second table: Walter Timmins, -?-, -?-, Kathleen Treadwell (standing with book), Ken Smith, Linda ?, Pat Marsh. *(Pat Darby)*

Pupils from All Saints' Church of England School celebrating May Day on the Old Church Vicarage lawn, *c.* 1956. Among those at the back are Sidney Oakley and Ann Law. Front row, left to right: -?-, Wilfred Timmins, John Robert Hall, Lesley Bradley, Pat Marsh, -?-, Denise Cartwright, -?-, Diane Horton, Kathleen Treadwell, Hazel Kent, Jennifer Morris, -?-. *(Pat Darby)*

All Saints' senior school netball team, 1962/63. Back row, left to right: Muriel Pike, Maureen Gibbs, Linda Thompson, Katherine Shipley, Frank Garrett. Front row: Jean Hudson, Pat Marsh, Kathleen Treadwell, Diane Goodby, Christine Handley. *(Pat Darby)*

All Saints' senior school netball team, 1951/52. Back row, left to right: Marion Ceney, Brenda Lovatt, Sheila Smith, Barbara Powell. Front row: Doreen Davies, Iris Corfield, Jean Holder. *(Sheila Swan)*

Class 5 at Black Lake Infants and Junior School, *c.* 1931. Only two pupils are known on this picture: Don Coles seated third from the right, second row, and Ray Markham seated second from the left, front row. The teacher standing in front of the door is Lee Dodd who was also a player/member of West Bromwich Dartmouth Cricket Club. *(Ray Markham)*

A Beeches Road School play, *c.* 1953. Back row, left to right: Christine Barker, June Britton, -?-, Gillian Watson, Maureen Evitts, -?-, -?-. Among the middle row: Alan Winwood, Berkley Flemming, Brian Cooper, John Stevens, Peter Dangerfield, David Woodcock, Malcolm Wakeman, Jill Tuckey. Front row: Carol Moore, -?-, -?-, Margaret Williams, -?-, -?-, Barbara Wesson. *(Carol Reynolds)*

Beeches Road junior mixed school country dance festival entrants pictured at the Adelphi Ballroom, New Street, West Bromwich, summer 1949. Back row, left to right: -?-, -?-, Gwenda Briggs, -?-, -?-, Joyce Johnson, ? Timmins, -?-, ? Thomas, -?-, ? Johnson, ? Lloyd. Middle row: Sylvia Knight, Frances Treadwell, Betty Hall, -?-, Sylvia Nock, -?-, Barbara ?, -?-, -?-, Megan Lloyd, -?-, -?-, Miss K.M. Boult. Front row: Joan Gardiner, Joyce Ashcroft, Sheila Curzon, Maisie Lovell, Dorothy Winston, -?-, Christine Smith. (*Frances Davies*)

Form 1, Bratt Street School, 1932. Back row, left to right: ? Siddons, Arthur Moreton, Eric Fieldhouse, Frank Pinfold, Lionel Roberts, Ernie Timmins, -?-, Reg Kramer, Ted Bytheway, Norman Perkins. Among the fourth row: Ray Johnson, Colin Mansell, Ernie Longhurst, Geoffrey Fieldhouse, ? Poultney. Third row: -?-, Fred Herbert, Lewis Lowe, Arthur Wilkins, ? Sadler, Jack Callaghan, Norman Grice, -?-, Ernie Lees, ? James, Ron Hadland. Fifth in the second row: Laurie Simmons. Front row: Tommy Chancellor, Alec Straughan, Donald Bridge, Norley Warren, Donald Jay. (*Eric Fieldhouse*)

Charlemont School FC, 1956/57. Back row, left to right: Michael Woodward, Billy Cox, George Banner. Middle row: Ray Bisseker, Peter Bell, Ken Broadbent, Trevor Garman. Front row: Ken Rogers, Alan Shepherd, Joe Cowles, Ken Sherwood, Bobby Bates. *(Trevor Garman)*

Charlemont School infants class, *c.* 1950. Back row, left to right: Marjorie Babbs, Janet Goodwin, Martin Haynes, Pat Page, Douglas Cope, Geraldine Skidmore, Graham Woodley, -?-, Norman Gould, Jackie Bunn, Bill Boucher, Margaret Udall, Mabel Davies. Third row: Michael Woodward, Christine Baggott, Michael Broadbent, -?-, John Bailey, Anne Carless, Trevor Clifton, Marion Davies, Tony Wright, Barbara King, Bernard Shenton, Margaret Redrup, Ray Cliff. Second row: David Branson, Pam Millard, Don Fitzpatrick, Val Hale, Roy Franks, Maureen Watkins, Barry Shepherd, Susan Smith, Michael Edmunds, Brenda Woodcock, Phil Slater. Front row: Pam Bevan, Susan ?, Margaret Dixon, Val Wiseman, Tony Fitzpatrick, Pauline Parkes, Margaret Garratt, -?-, June Rose. *(Roy Franks)*

Charlemont School infants class, *c.* 1950. Back row, left to right: Mabel Davies, Eric Baker, Margaret Cook, Gordon Morton, Judith Neale, Alan Jones, Angela Turton, Derek Nelson, Margaret Whitehouse, David Smith, Barbara McNair, Timothy Wharton, Christine Onions. Third row: Margaret Knott, Trevor ?, Veronica Gardner, Roy Westwood, Edwina Bowater, Douglas Parish, Kathleen Coggins, Malcolm Judge, Pat Gould, Gerald Dyer, Vivien Ault, George Walton, Sylvia Langley. Second row: David Woodman, Susan Gooding, Godfrey Turley, Joy Harris, Barry Howes, Sylvia Reading, Tony Marson, Barbara Cooksey, Roger Holden, Lynn Millward, David ?. Front row: June Darling, Helen Brokhouse, Alan Davis, May Gordon, Dennis Healey, Gloria Fernihough, Pat Myhill, Wendy Fitzpatrick. *(Susan Nock)*

Churchfield School FC, *c.* 1970. Back row, left to right: Steven Moore, Brian Lewis, Kevin Blackhall, Brian Davies, Barry Rotton, Chris Cuthbert, Steven Ash. Front row: John Stokes, Michael Reed, Steve Lynex, David Boughton, Chris Morris. Steve Lynex went on to become a professional football player with a number of clubs including Leicester City and West Bromwich Albion. Out of ten first team appearances for the Baggies he scored just one goal, in a 2–2 draw with Sunderland at the Hawthorns on 4 April 1987. His career total, however, was 70 goals in more than 400 games. *(David Boughton)*

Cronehills Selective Central Girls School, form 1A, 1932. Back row, left to right: -?-, Margaret ?, ? Robinson, Jean Warden, -?-, ? Banner, -?-, ? Saunders, -?-, Marion Stevens. Third row, second from left: Beatrice Hoare. Second row: -?-, -?-, Evelyn Allmark, Joan Williams, Miss Chandler, Madeleine Hall, -?-, -?-, Irene Hoare, -?-. Front row: Evelyn Walters, Elizabeth ?, Margaret Aston, Minnie Faizey, Ivy Hood, Sheila Pugh, -?-, -?-, Adelaide Ramsdale, Priscilla ?. *(Margaret Sargent)*

Cronehills Selective Central Boys School, Form 1A, 1932. Back row, sixth and eighth from left: Roy Deeley, Des Moore. Fourth row, first and third from left: Mr F.A. Harding (headmaster), Eric Fieldhouse. Third row, first and third from right: Stan Greenhalgh, Ernest Timmins. Second row: -?-, -?-, Cyril Banyard, -?-, Bob Cashmore, -?-, Douglas Edwards, Sam Pugh. Front row: -?-, Frank Pennington, -?-, Jack Callaghan, Norman Grice, -?-. *(Eric Fieldhouse)*

Cronehills Secondary Technical Boys School prefects, *c.* 1947. Back row, left to right: Frank Gibbs, Derek Parkes, Jim Corbett, Bob Ralphs, Ray Gould, Derek Morgan. Middle row: David Kendrick, Dennis Denning, Bob Pitwood, Robert Horton, Bob Arnold, Ernest 'Eppie' Parker. Front row: Ray Powell, -?-, Geoff Moxey. This building opened in 1925 as a selective central school and became a secondary technical in 1947. *(Bob Ralphs)*

Cronehills Selective Central Girls School, *c.* 1945. Back row, left to right: Moira Richardson, Jean Reynolds, Mabel Ramsdale, Heather Payton, Joyce Lester, June Green, Rita Frost, Eileen Jeavons, -?-, Valerie Higgs, Dorothy Hale. Fourth row: -?-, Evelyn Smith, Evelyn Ricketts, Ivy Williams, Ivy Burns. Third row: Sheila Henson, Margaret Partridge, Joan Mansell, Margaret Harthill, -?-, -?-, Gwyneth Aston, Freda ?, -?-, Brenda Fereday, -?-. Second row: Beryl Hayes, Jean Finch, Pam Clarke, Barbara Allerton, Brenda Downing, Miss Satchwell. Front row: Margaret Wootton, Freda Wilkes, Annie Taylor, Jean Richardson, Pauline Stanton. *(Annie Willis)*

Fisher Street Infants and Junior school, *c.* 1934. Back row, left to right: Doreen Worley, Irene Melia, Brian Fellows, -?-. Third row: Alan Brookes, Iris Shadbourne, Donald Hill, Iris Vanes. Second row: Dorothy Williams, Aileen Mincher, Barbara Shepherd, Irene Price, Barbara Nicklin, Ann Henshaw, Gwen Fardell. Front row: Ronnie Stubbs, Raymond Foster, Geoffrey Noot. *(Aileen Whitehouse)*

Fisher Street Infants and Junior School, *c.* 1936. The school was built on the West Bromwich side of Great Bridge in 1859 to serve the nearby Wesleyan Methodist Chapel, which curiously was situated in the Tipton Parish. Following the transfer to local authority control in 1907 the senior pupils were, in 1932, moved to the new George Salter School in West Bromwich. Fisher Street School finally closed in 1969. Back row, left to right: Irene James, Irene Davies, Gwen Emms, Beryl Douglas, Gertie Gilbert, Grace Reynolds. Middle row: Lizzie Oliver, Ida Stokes, Nora Meredith, Mary Wootton, Gladys Bratt. Front row: Hilda Bratt, Joyce Whitehouse, Ethel Riley, Gwen Davies, Olive Wilkes. *(Laurence Dow)*

Fisher Street Infants and
Junior school, *c.* 1924.
On the left: Mr Morris
(teacher). Third row, third
from left: Eva ?. Second
row, first from left: Sarah
Bates, first from right, Hilda
Palfreyman. Front row: Doris
George, Phyllis Banner, Gwen
Duggan, Beulah Wilkinson.
(Doris Hall)

Greets Green Junior School
FC, 1957. Back row, left
to right: Thomas George
Summerton, Gerwyn Price.
Third row: Ray Taft, Roy
Groves, Brian Walford, Roy
Geddes, Ken Law, Colin Male.
Second row: Brian Page,
Peter Wright, Ernie Hughes,
John Baker, Geoff Garratt.
Front row: Colin Smith,
Robert Carter. *(Ernie Hughes)*

Pupils at Greets Green Junior
School making model rockets
in July 1970, an end-of-term
activity. This was possibly
to commemorate the first
moon landing by American
astronauts, which took place
on 16 July 1969. From left
to right: Ian Fisher, Peter
Norton, Diane Jukes, Dean
Barnes, Graham Astley.
(George Barnes)

George Salter Secondary Modern Boys School intermediate football team, *c.* 1955. Back row, left to right: Brian Wilkes, David Holland, Alan Male, Barry Cashmore, Tony Doody, Tommy Pearsall, Barry Parker, Leslie Oldhams. Front row: Harry Fletcher, Geoffrey Evans, Michael Postans, Reg Turley (headmaster), John Hartley, Bobby Weston, Barry Fellows. *(Brian Wilkes)*

George Salter Secondary Modern Girls School netball team pictured in the assembly hall, autumn 1951. Back row, left to right: Joyce Whitehouse, Joyce Pitt, Gwen Nason, Sheila Powell. Front row: Brenda Botfield, Anne Harrison, Doreen Edmunds. *(Joyce Smith)*

George Salter High School third year football team, 1970/71. Back row, left to right: Michael Butler, John Fellows, Keith Vickerstaff, Paul Rees, Michael King, Sammy ?. Front row: -?-, Kirk Ebanks, Abtar Singh, John Ricketts, Ian Bayliss, -?-, Shaun Withington. *(Dorothy Ricketts)*

George Salter Secondary Modern Girls School, form 2B, *c.* 1950. Back row, left to right: Anne Woodbine, Audrey Simcox, Doreen Bolton, Enid Dyke. Third row: Monica Benbow, ? Nock, Freda ?, Kay ?, Brenda Barnfield, -?-, -?-, -?-. Second row: -?-, ? Price, -?-, Judy Doleman, Cynthia Weston, Janet ?, -?-, -?-, Joyce Abbott, Barbara Marriott, Olive Tycer. Front row: Pauline Botfield, -?-, Ann Wells, Joan Clarke, -?-, Ruth Stampe, Ivy Lissimore, -?-, -?-, Doreen Carter. *(Doreen Shannon)*

George Salter Secondary Modern Boys School, 1949. In the back row, from left to right: Ray Whale, Ken Wilkinson. Fifth row: Alf Broadbent, Harry Bennett. Fourth row: Billy Marriott, Ken Dugmore, Colin Jones, Sam Copson, Ernie Holmes, Bill Ferguson, Fred Rackham. Third row: Ivor Bratt, Les Whitehouse, Les Walker, Stuart Morton, Gordon Taylor. Front row: Frank Roberts, -?-, -?-, Arthur Powell, John Bromley, -?-, Derek Reynolds, -?- , -?-, -?-. *(T.J.H. Price)*

George Salter Secondary Modern Girls School, form IIIE, March 1955. Back row, left to right: Sheila Brookes, -?-, Gladys Pincher, Georgina Horton, Hazel ?, Marlene Graham, Freda Pitt, Doreen Cox, Hazel Simms, Hilary Baker, Pearl Stephens. Middle row: Doreen Timmins, Olive Tinsley, Pauline Bradnick, Judith Morris, Barbara Pearce, -?-. Front row: Margaret Burton, Mary Fryer, Doris ?, Joan Cadman. *(Judith John)*

George Salter Secondary Modern Boys School cross country team, *c.* 1952. Back row, left to right: Arthur Brown, Brian Pritchard, John Baker, Keith Herbert, Brian Percival, David Thompson, Brian Darby, Geoff Watkins, Tom Meek. Front row: Tony Moore, Ron Welch, Tony Harris, Tony Welch, David Rushton, Edward Richardson, Geoff Morris, Billy Mills, Keith Waller, Geoff Williams. *(Mary Pattison)*

George Salter Secondary Modern Girls School, form IIIE, 1953. Back row, left to right: Gillian Clements, Glenys Owen, Margaret Fereday, Evelyn Beattie, Ivy Withers, Pat Copson, Christine East, Ann Farley, Jill ?, Linda Markham. Third row: Pauline Moore, Mary Broome, Janet Nevey, Linda Durnall, Mavis Attwell, Audrey Connor, Maureen Smith. Second row: Celia Hill, Valerie Green, Jean Shellard, Janet Sinar, June Ralley, Janet Fellows, Helen Cox. Front row: Jean Newbold, -?-, Brenda Mills, Joan Collins, Sylvia Weston, -?-, Joyce Arter. *(Maureen Lippitt)*

George Salter Secondary Modern Girls School, form 2X, 1955. Back row, left to right: Carol White, Brenda Banks, Pauline Davies, Christa Matthews, Rita Wells, Margaret Riley. Third row: Betty Matthews, Pat Morgan, Sheila Moore, Ann Hickinbottom, Iris Langford, Margaret Markham, Christine Stokes, Brenda Bradley, Ann Johnson, Sheila Lockley, Marlene Franks. Second row: Jean Wheatley, Jean Whitehouse, Linda Stevens, Jean Pritchard, Valerie Dyke, Valerie Ives. Front row: Barbara Bradley, Janet Sadler, Beryl Whitehouse, Pauline Sadler, Beryl Thompson, Barbara Jordan, Sheila Keogh, Doreen Bedward. *(Jean Edmunds)*

Alderman Jack Williams, Mayor of West Bromwich, presents the cycling proficiency trophy to head boy John Somerfield and head girl Gillian Dell at Gorse Farm Junior School, Great Barr, March 1972. Head-mistress Miss J. Lunn announced that the school had gained the award at their first attempt with sixty out of seventy entrants passing the test. Left to right: Alderman Jack Williams, John Somerfield, Gillian Dell. *(Jack Williams)*

Guns Village Primary Girls School, 1948. Back row, ninth and tenth from the left: Sheila Norris, Doreen Ainsbury. Third row: Brenda Barnfield, Kay ?, Doreen Bolton, Pauline ?, Irene Shepherd, -?-, Sylvia Lowe, -?-, Barbara Jones, Pauline Plant, -?-, Clare Mitchell (teacher). Second row, first and third: Sheila Smith, Jean Carpenter. Front row: -?-, -?-, Enid Dyke, ? Grice, -?-. *(Doreen Shannon)*

Grove Vale School football team, 1970/71. Back row, left to right: Mike Rowledge, Steven Carter, Anthony Firkin, Paul Bailey (teacher), Nigel Taylor, Chris Nunns, Mark Whitmore, Perry Ewens. Front row: David Smith, Neil Tucker, Anthony Boughton, Peter Smith, John Clorley, John Bissell. *(Anthony Boughton)*

Guns Village Primary Girls School, 1946. Back row, left to right: Brenda Burkitt, Doreen Armstrong, -?-, -?-, Eunice Hale, Mary Hale, Margaret Burton, -?-, Joyce Abbotts, Sheila Spicer, -?-, Nora Clayton, -?-. Third row: Winifred Finney, Eileen Berrow, Betty Jeavons, Mary Russell, Margaret Hunt, Sheila Hodgetts, Joan Mitchell, Margaret Price, Betty Beattie, Pamela Phillips, Pat Evans, Sheila Haynes. Second row: Joyce Jeavons, Barbara Timmins, Janet Morgan, Beryl Day, Madeline Corbett, Sylvia Richards, Joan Fisher, Rita Daffon, -?-, Gladys ?, Janet Wheatley, Betty Simms, Madge Warley. Front row: Sylvia Hale, Janet Whatmore, -?-, Delma Brierley, Ethel Turton, Brenda Dixon, Norma Smith, Gladys Slater, Pat Brown. *(Mary Partridge)*

Guns Village Primary Mixed School, 1956. Back row, left to right: Robert Lewis, David Malborn, Keith Belmore, Laurence Farley, Judith Hutchinson, Gwen Richards, Ian Macleod, Valerie Wilkinson, Daryl Lloyd, Keith Langford, Michael Harrison, Sandra Inns, Stephen Cadman. Middle row: Alan Whitehouse, Gillian Newman, Margaret Stewart, -?-, Hazel Pitt, Viven ?, Jacqueline Keys, Pauline Mullany, Jane Evans, Carol Lord, June ?, David Townsend. Front row: -?-, David Badger, Gordon Judge, Malcolm Griffiths, Dorothy Griffiths, -?-, Robert Frier, Peter Austin, Constance ?, Robert Jones, Peter ?, Ronald Beckett, Judith Minchin. *(David Malborn)*

West Bromwich Grammar School FC, 1948/49. Back row, left to right: Doug Hodges, Eric Peters, Derek Healey, Fred Onions, Jim Patterson, Joe Lole, Harry Wright, Harry Deeley. Front row: Alan Oakes, Derek Schnabel, John Beattie, Paul Dennis, Ron Coley. *(Graham Woodall)*

West Bromwich Grammar School inter-house sports day held on Newton Road playing fields, *c.* 1957. Among the crowd: Catherine Williams, Gillian Reynolds, Marion Law, Sylvia Langley, Diana Cliff, Pauline Brown, Vivien Watts, Pat Shelton, June Lissimore, Brenda Hale, Selwyn Hayward, Doreen Faulkner, Valerie Turner, Mervyn Hughes, Pat Lodge, Eunice Randle, Bob Dale, Philip Russell, Janet Reynolds. *(Graham Woodall)*

Gilbert and Sullivan's *Iolanthe* performed by the pupils of West Bromwich Grammar School, March 1969. Back row, left to right: Geoffrey Franklin, Robert Williams, David Payne, Gilbert Darby, David Ingram, Vaughan Wilkinson, John Stubbs, Graham Woodall, Andrew Wharton, Tony Griffiths, Geoffrey Reader, Martin James. Middle row: Derek Williams, Anne Whittingham, Barbara Lane, Kim Woodward, Molly Thomas, Anne Riseborough, Judith Perkins, Jane Brown, Jeannette Rasmusson, Christine Evans, Christine Tyler, Elizabeth Robottom, Sheila Hall, Julia Millerchip, Celia Marston, Sheila Norgove. Front row: Lynne Chisholme, Elaine Daniel, Steve Turton, Margaret Parsons, John Worton, Janet Gwilliam, Trevor Smith, Roderick Keyes, Lisbeth Brown, Roger Rowbotham, Stephanie Cox. *(Graham Woodall)*

West Bromwich Grammar School, form 5S, c. 1941. Back row, left to right: Peter Foakes, -?-, Stuart Cole, Hedley Graham German. Middle row: -?-, ? Williams, ? Jones, Clive Wharton, Dorian Russell, Haulwen Lort. Front row: Irene Starr, Jean Pickering, Mary Kimberley, Marguerite Luxon, Marie Russell, Marguerite Lowry. (Graham Woodall)

West Bromwich Municipal Secondary School, form 4A, c. 1934. Back row, left to right: Jack Williams, Stan Prince, Alan Nicholls, -?-, Jack Shaw, Harry Stubbs, Tommy Jordan, Norman Williams, Arnold Bennett, Harold Baker. Middle row: Mary Wharton, Miriam Jackson, Edith Baker, Joan Rudge, Vera Horton, Dorothy Stamps, Edna Dixon, Marjorie Thornhill, Marion Bennett. Front row: Frank Jones, Frank Wootton, Nora Armstrong, Doreen Davies, Frederick 'Charlie' Walton, Marjorie Thomas, Dorothy Tack, Phyllis Poxon, George Leadbeater, Stan Page. (Vera Horton)

George Bernard Shaw's *Arms and the Man* performed by pupils of West Bromwich Grammar School, December 1968. Back row, left to right: Margaret Hill, Arthur Kellitt, Tony Pitt, Michael Whitman, Margaret Pitt. Middle row: John Perry, Stephen Young, Margaret Parsons, Carol Holman-Smith, Wayne Luckman, Kevin Treadwell, Olive Robins, Elaine Daniels, Stephen Northover, Peter Jennings. Front row: Dennis Walker, Ann Millward, David Ingram, Clare Perry, John Fox, Jacqueline Grice, Michael Skerrett, Graham Wootton. *(Beryl Wootton)*

West Bromwich Grammar School, form 1C, June 1940. Back row, left to right: Laurence Jones, Geoffrey Allen, Jack Neale, ? Morris, -?-, Gordon Rushton, -?-, ? Biddulph, ? Page. Third row: Brian Duckworth, Jean Whitmore, Doreen Lane, Mary Spruce, Doreen Carswell, -?-, Mary Mitchell, Dorothy Reynolds, ? Holland. Second row: Elsie Downes, Joan Rushton, Elva Herring, Bertha Walwyn, Jeanne Tempest, -?-, Mary Bowen, June Tranter, Joan Southall. Front row: Selwyn Hares, Geoffrey Richards. *(Jack Neale)*

West Bromwich Grammar School, form 4L, 1943. Back row, left to right: Alan Brookes, Brian Wood, Alan Webster, Eric Carpenter. Middle row: Frank Bryant, Alan Garratt, George Johns, Ken Bissell, Nancy Walker, Alison Barlow, John Hill, Eric Williams. Front row: Jean Cooper, Iris Vanes, Maisey Newey, Valerie Pegg, Frederick 'Charlie' Walton, Mary Cooksey, Irene Howes, Marion Williams, Kathleen Bridge. *(Iris Gill)*

West Bromwich Grammar School inter-house sports day winners, Olympians, pictured at their Birmingham Road venue on Saturday 15 July 1950. Back row, left to right: Bill Cruise, Horace Cockcroft, Cllr Arthur Medley, Jessie Medley, Derek Carter, Michael Chatwin, Geoff Robinson. Front row: Kenneth Graham, Winifred Jones, Iris Williams, Derek Schnabel, Corinne Hughes, Lawrence Aulton, Valerie Owen, Alan Hayward, Peter Pritchard. *(Lawrence Aulton)*

West Bromwich Grammar School, *c.* 1946. Back row, left to right: Gordon Jukes, Ron Blackburn, ? Moore, Laurie Lawrence, Paul Dennis, -?-, Harry Farmer, Geoff Hawkins. Middle row: -?-, Laurence Lees, -?-, Jim Patterson, -?-, -?-, -?-, -?-, Lawrence Aulton, Dennis Evans, John Edgington. Front row: Jennifer Hardy, ? Shenton, -?-, -?-, -?-, Harry 'Sam' Welch, -?-, Pat Holloway, Sheila Barton, Betty Billingham, -?-. *(Jenny Edwards)*

West Bromwich Municipal Secondary School, form 5L, *c.* 1938. Back row, left to right: John Potter, Ken Westbury, Jeff Thompson, Frank Crump, Reg Foakes, Arthur Reeves, Clive Wharton, -?-. Middle row: Albert Stokes, -?-, Robert Smith, Alan Rawsthorne, Ken Brookes, Joan Baggott, Eileen Jones, Douglas Barnbrook, Irene Smith. Front row: Elsie Malaise, Kathleen Stringer, Azalea Enid Gwilliam, Frederick 'Charlie' Walton, Betty Vowles, Johanna Manley, Irene Stanfield, Maisie Cole. *(Joan Oldhams)*

West Bromwich Grammar School, form 1C, 1941. Back row, left to right: John Austin, Mike Thornton, Ken Cartwright, Stanley Amos, ? Greaves, John Wheatley, John Lones, Alfred Darby, ? Richards, Peter Weldon. Third row: John Broom, Geoffrey Green, Anita Bonas, Betty Green, Joy Morris, Sheila Sorrell, Olive Onions, Mary Paggett, Stanley Blackwell, Edgar Bloor. Second row: Phyllis Cooper, Mavis Aulton, Beryl Green, Mona Knowles, Bertha Walwyn, Margaret Allen, Jean Morris, Kathleen Downing, Betty Hares. Front row: Eric Matchett, Eric Dickins, Roland Hill, Frank Grice, Roger Lord. *(Lawrence Aulton)*

West Bromwich Grammar School, form 5L, *c.* 1942. Back row, left to right: Fred Neville, ? Hughes, John Davies, Bill Squire, Geoffrey Haynes, Peter Stevens, Jeffrey Symonds. Front row: Freda Coombes, Tessa Sower, Dorothy Hobbs, Margaret Blackwell, Francis 'Jacko' Jackson, Iris Newey, Muriel Brown, Florence Croton, Alan Moore. *(Graham Woodall)*

West Bromwich Grammar School, form 5S, *c.* 1942. Back row, left to right: Roger Anstey, Norman Knight, Michael Ford, Robert 'Ginger' Parkes, Jack Standing. Middle row: John Llewellyn, Ben Whale, Bill Cooper, Geoff Haywood, Bill Udall, Stan Duggard. Front row: Dennis Badhams, Marion Kershaw, Freda Griffiths, Betty Nightingale, Lucy 'Cat' Harris, Roy Dixon, -?-, Maurice Everley, Ron Moore. *(Graham Woodall)*

West Bromwich Grammar School, form 2B, 1942. Back row, left to right: Stanley Amos, Ken Cartwright, John Brewes, John Wheatley, Roland Hill, Eric Matchett, Stanley Blackwell, -?-, Ray Holland, Selwyn Hares. Third row: Geoff Green, Howard Parker, Edwin Turton, Peggy Teague, Betty Hares, Barbara Richards, Kathleen Downing, Mary Woods, Roger Lord, Arthur Head. Second row: Barbara Johnson, Mavis Aulton, Norma Johnson, Doris Hawkins, Gwen Evans, Sheila Princep, Eileen Edwards, Rachel Griffin, Mona Knowles. Front row: Ken Edwards, Dennis Carpenter, Donald Farmer, -?-, Kelvin Coldicott, Geoffrey Beardsmore. *(Lawrence Aulton)*

Hamstead Infants and Junior School, form 5, *c.* 1951. Back row, left to right, first, second, eleventh, fourteenth: Mary Lissimore, Elsa Pearsall, Mary ?, Christine Onions. Second row: Barbara Prince, Linda Cooper, Veronica Cooper, -?-, -?-, -?-, Mary Fletcher, Priscilla Cheese, -?-, -?-, Sandra Rollingson, -?-, -?-, -?-. *(Linda Heeley)*

Hamstead Infants and Junior School, *c.* 1953. Back row, left to right: Reg Jones, Sandra Cheesman, Christine Davies, Sandra Care, Margaret Wrigley, Gillian Webb, Carol Stevens, Jennifer Taylor, Sandra Pasmore, -?-, -?-. Third row: Maxine Smith, Virginia Tolley, Janet Price, Barbara Harris, Janice Hall, Diane Guest, Valerie ?, -?-, Rosemary Rowley, Marilyn Moore, -?-, -?-, Linda Whittaker. Second row: -?-, Barbara Prince, Linda Cooper, Pat Billings, Pat Scott, Sandra Summerfield, Priscilla Cheese, Iris Pearsall, Janet Allen, Rita Priest, Christine Marsh, Sandra Clark. Front row: Linda Kendrick, Jean Goodchild, Joan Poynton, -?-, -?-, -?-, -?-, Jacqueline Gregory, -?-, Carol ?. *(Linda Heeley)*

Hamstead Infants and Junior School, *c.* 1946. Back row, left to right: Frank Wootton, Willis Chandler, Geoffrey Ball, Ron Jones, Ken Hill, Barry Woolaston, John Westwood, Gilbert ?, Terry Blackwell, Donald Snadden, Tony Guest, Terry Connop, Jack Shipley. Third row: Iris ?, Margaret Jones, -?-, Alice Osell, -?-, ? Wilkins, Jean Snadden, June Round, -?-, Pam Gittens, June Patterson, Rosalind Scott, ? Stevens, -?-, ? Mitchell. Second row: Michael Blogg, Jennifer Houghton, Sheila Salt, -?-, Barbara Wedgbury, Reg Jones, Audrey Tolley, Pauline Blunn, Sheila Rushton, Sheila Keasey, Colin Fortnam. Front row: -?-, -?-, -?-, John Keach, Marion Bradbury, Maurice Ash, -?-, James Freeth, ? Cooper, Robert Golding, Mavis Totney. *(Colin Fortnam)*

Three Wise Men bearing gifts in a scene from the Christmas nativity play performed by pupils of Hamstead Infants and Junior School, *c.* 1958. Back row, left to right: Victoria Ford, Jane Whitehead, -?-, Susan Leedham, -?-. Front row: -?-, -?-. *(Carol Leedham)*

Hateley Heath Junior School football team, 1962/63. Back row, left to right: Ron Burton, Neil Jones, Graham Woodall, Tommy Walker, Michael Westwood, Malcolm Ford, Peter Hunt, John Smith. Front row: Geoff Allen, Ron Cooper, Philip Brookes, Philip Mogg, Bobby Shinton. In a career spanning eleven years from 1972 Bobby Shinton played professional football for Walsall, Wrexham, Millwall and Newcastle scoring 99 league goals in almost 400 games. *(Graham Woodall)*

Hateley Heath Junior School, class 4C, *c.* 1952. Back row, left to right: -?-, -?-, Colin Lloyd, Sidney Wheatley, Raymond Powell, Philip Cosnett. Third row: Geoff Hughes, David Peniket, Tony Cavell, Brian Bates, Terry Sims, Fred Harris, Jean Williams. Second row: John Reed, -?-, Sheila Hampson, -?-, ? Brookes, Terry Makepeace. Front row: Joan Secker, Jean Carter, Brenda Garbett, June Dudley, Jean Emms, -?-. *(Terry Sims)*

Hateley Heath Junior School football team, 1957/58. Back row, left to right: Terry Johnson, Tony Whitehouse, Roland Harper, John Workman, Brian Hampson. Middle row: John Burgess, Tony Richards, John Sims, John Knight, Alan Ledbury. Front row: Derek Davies, Archie Brookes. *(Terry Sims)*

Hateley Heath Junior School rounders team, 1967. Played 8, won 8. For: 83½ against: 22. Back row, left to right: Sylvia Brown, Monica Gordon, Karen Harvey, Doreen Henry, Ann Smith, Lee Hawker. Middle row: Margo Davison, Olwyn Burnell, Julie Morris, Judith Hodgetts, Vicky Evans. · Front row: Vivien Addis, Julie Clancey. *(Julie Wildman)*

Harvills Hawthorn Infants and Junior School pantomime, *Sleeping Beauty*, *c.* 1952. Back row, left to right: Albert Fendall, Brenda Munns, Valerie Webb, -?-. Third row: Victor Faulkner, Pauline Cartwright, Janet Bromley, Pat Stone, Barbara Phillpott, Pauline Webb, Joan Rolfe, -?-. Second row: Mavis Jones, Margaret Ceney, Margaret Buckley, Peter Cox, Joan Faulkner, Peter Phillips, Harold Devey, Carol Miles, -?-. Front row: June Clements, Joan Basford, Carol Badhams, Margaret Stevens. *(Pauline Cooper)*

Hall Green Infants and Junior School Christmas play, loosely based on the nativity, *c.* 1958. Back row, left to right: -?-, Julian Richardson, -?-. Middle row: -?-, ? Dunn, Graham Sheldon, -?-, -?-, -?-, Glynis Walton. Front row: Keith Beasley, John Bissell, Graham Wootton, Melvyn Colley. *(Betty Wootton)*

Hill Top Secondary Modern School choir, 1956. Among the back row, left to right: Donald Ferguson, Doug Baker, Michael Grainger, Geoff Nevey, Geoff Hughes, Ken Hawthorn, David Williams, Terry Upton. Third row: Ken Smith, John Walker, Alec Brookes, Philip Hartill, Robert Kingston, Graham Geddes, Tom Ruston, Bill Evans, Brian Day, Laurence Meadows, Ken Cartwright. Second row: Melvyn Gwynn, -?-, Trevor Duffield, Peter Nicholls, Philip Vaughan, -?-, -?-, John Jones, Barry Hampton, -?-, Brian Roberts, Tony Hartle, -?-, Trevor Perkins, Brian Peniket, Leslie Hunt. Front row: -?-, Derek Day, Bertram Pitt, John Jukes, George Burgess, -?-, Fred Bartram, Robert Bird, Barry Moseley, Sam Richards, Michael Ward, -?-, -?-. *(Trevor Perkins)*

Hill Top School Senior Football Club, 1956. Back row, left to right: Jack Lowe, Donald Ferguson, Melvyn Pugh, Leslie Fletcher, Bill Hodgkins, Colin Pittaway, Albert Mogg, Tom Powell. Middle row: Jeff Wheatley, Graham Mole, Alec Brookes, Malcolm Saunders, Arthur Brown, Philip Smith, ? Simms. Front row: Ken Smith, David Price. *(Leslie Fletcher)*

Hill Top senior inter-school athletic champions, 1958. Back row, left to right, Roy Turley, Geoff Chauner, Andrew Smith. Third row: ? Hadley, Stan Fletcher, Patrick Burton, Anthony Smith. Second row: Jack Lowe, ? Higgs, John Chatterton, Sam Richards, Jeff Wheatley, -?-, Leonard Mansell. Front row: Maurice Whitehouse, Brian Ford, Leslie Fletcher, Bill Hodgkins, David Bedenham, Graham Mole, Paul Timmins. *(Leslie Fletcher)*

Hill Top School Intermediate Football Club, 1956. Back row, left to right: Jack Lowe, -?-, Brian Mercer, David Bedenham, Sam Richards, Alan Shorthouse, Barry Hampton, Alan Stevens, Tom Powell. Middle row: Stan Fletcher, Tom Doleman, Alan Hodgkins, John Price, Frank Hartle, Keith Lloyd, Trevor Perkins. Front row: Brian Peniket, Keith Jones. *(Trevor Perkins)*

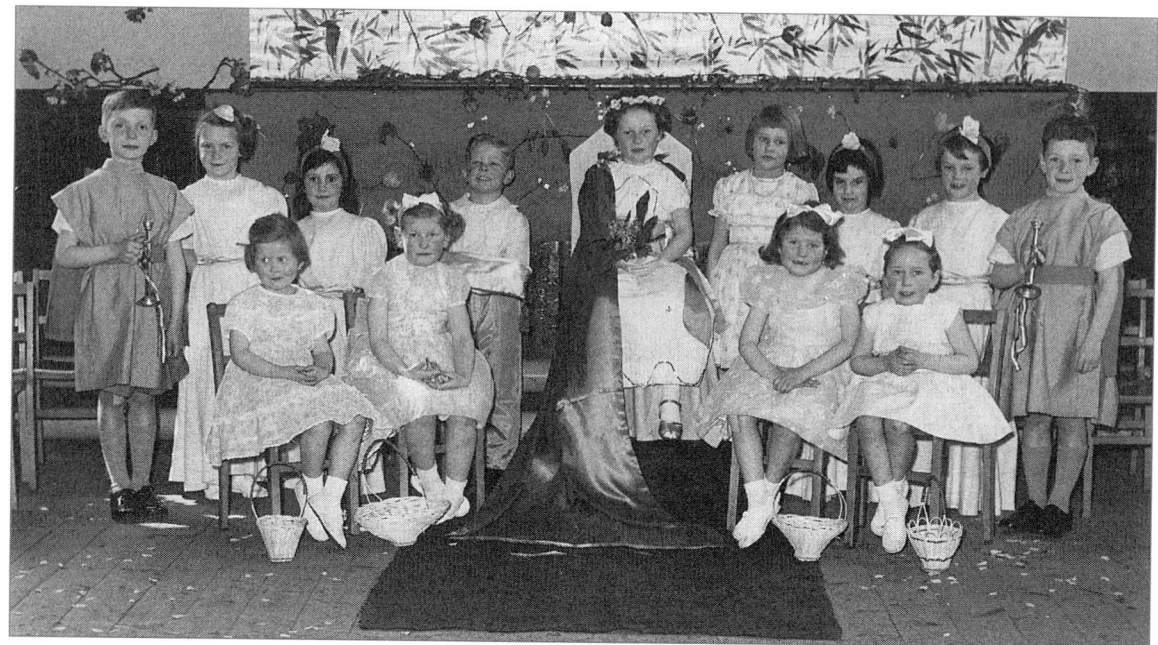

Holy Trinity Infants and Junior School May Queen, 1960. Back row, left to right: Ashley Ludgate, Lynn Francis, Anita Turner, Robert Willan, June Baker, Susan Willan, Pamela Edwards, Pamela Haycock, Ken ?. Front row: Diane Holland, Susan Jennings, Lorraine Groves, Jacqueline Bates. *(Joan Haycock)*

Holy Trinity Infants and Junior School, 1951. Back row, left to right: Tom Crisp, Geoffrey Horne, Brian ?, Terence Arnold, Ken Tuck, Michael Partridge. Brian Robinson, Reg Beasley, Michael Garbett, Albert Barnfield, Peter Lloyd, Dennis Edwards, Bill Cotton, Gary Botfield ? Morris. Third row: June Freer, Pat ?, Jeanette Reynolds, Janet Yates, Dorothy Reece, Jill Davies, Ann Duffield, Maureen Orme, Pat Butwell, Pat Scott, Sylvia Charlton, Pauline Martin. Second row: Fred Evitts, John Harris, Brenda Cooper, Judith Bowen, Sulamit Brown, Doreen Faulkner, Joyce Hughes, Christine Howen, Maxine Martin, June Wilkes, Mavis Draper, John Payne, Philip Whitehouse. Front row: Robert ?, Terry Deeming, John Holmes, Keith Aspley, John Cherrington. *(Janet Baker)*

Holy Trinity Infants and Junior School, 1964. Back row, left to right: David Holland, -?-, Alan Harris, -?-, Peter Gibson, John Collins, Chris Mason, -?-, Brindley Mason, -?-. Third row: Surinder Kaur, Gillian Lee, Jacqueline Kay, Anita Foster, Alison Docker, -?-, ? Jenkins, -?-, Margaret Roden, Shirley Wilson, Frances ?, -?-, -?-, Lorraine Groves. Second row: Ann Dixon, ? Billingham, Susan Ferris, Susan Hollingsworth, Ivor Hodgetts, Tom Crisp, Linda Brown, -?-, -?-, Tanya Beattie. Front row: Robert Willan, ? Sago, -?-, John Simpson, Guy Millington, Sundar Singh, Robert Standing, -?-. *(Alison Reed)*

Holy Trinity Infants and Junior School, c. 1963. Back row, left to right: -?-, -?-, Stuart Groom, Sula ?, Sandra Holland, Pamela Haycock, Josephine Cox, Phyllis Hadley, Bernard Nock, Alan Simpson, Ashley Ludgate. Third row: -?-, Margaret Smith, Lynn Farmer, Deborah Robinson, Glynis Smith, Elaine Griffiths, Linda Brookes, -?-, Margaret Horton, Susan Ward, Lesley Bell. Second row: Louise Price, Janet Billingham, Lynn Francis, -?-, Ivor Hodgetts, Tom Crisp, Shirley Breakwell, Pamela Edwards, Patricia Parkes, -?-, -?-. Front row: Philip Burgess, David Billingham, -?-, -?-, Patrick Botfield, -?-, Christopher ?, -?-, Norman Ferris, Roy Freeman, -?-, Keith Tinsley. *(Joan Haycock)*

Joseph Edward Cox School, infants class 3, 1938. Back row, first, fourth and thirteenth from left: Miss Palmer, George Burkitt, Miss Lawrence. Third row, second, eleventh and thirteenth: Audrey Betts, Doris Dwyer, Miriam Brewer. Second row, ninth: Muriel Wilkes. Front row, first: Bernard Stamps. *(Miriam Smith)*

Joseph Edward Cox Junior School class, 1958. Back row, left to right: June Sumner, Linda Gaynor, Hazel Atterbury, Philip Hazelhurst, -?-, Tony Keir, -?-, Bruce Gopsil, Thomas Morgan, -?-, Raymond Short, John Green, Tony Baker. Third row: June Nock, Margaret Giles, Linda Parry, Barbara Bingham, Rita Wilde, Kathleen Isherwood, Irene Wallis, Brenda Osell, Jill Heath, Beryl Bayliss, Pat Cox, Jill Morris. Second row: -?-, Philip Huggins, -?-, Maurice Riley, Michael Hammond, -?-, Ron Smith, Brenda Johnson, Carol Barnfield, Joan Woodfield, Pat Wood, Janice Farmer, Thelma Simmons. Front row: Derek Compton, -?-, John Williams, Frank White, Raymond Jones, Colin Nicholls, Bernard Cooper, Philip Allen, Fred Smith, Michael Carswell. *(Barbara Perkins)*

Lodge Estate Infants and Junior School merit class, 1931. Back row, left to right: Philip Simmonds, Dennis Finch, -?-, Stan Wilkins, Norman Pearson, William Holding, Stan Jones, -?-, Eric Thiswell, Bobby Carter, ? Evans. Fourth: H.G. Cook, Jack Aspin, -?-, Dennis Beardsley, Harry Waldron, ? Whitehouse, Stan Beasley, Dennis Thatcher, Tom Ward, Robert Bowcott, Dennis Atkinson. Third: Tom Frowen, Leslie Thornhill, Dennis Turner, ? Bates, Dennis Moore, Raymond Gwynn, Lewis Marston, Tom Poole, Norman Edwards, ? Evans, Tom Walker, Jack Darby, Tom Malin. Second: Jack Houston, Dennis Ingram, Arnold Bird, Harry Darby, Tom Whale, -?-, Clarence Abraham, Stan Howard, Tom Emms. Front row: -?-, Ernie Brindley, -?-, Douglas Thomas, Norman Tinsley, Jack Spittle, -?-, Jack Wildon. *(Tom Malin)*

Lodge Estate Infants and Junior School, *c.* 1956. Back row, ninth and tenth from left: Carol Winsper, Mildred Bisseker. Middle row: -?-, -?-, -?-, Valerie Smith, Rosemary Sewell, -?-, -?-, Pat Nock, June Ricketts, -?-, -?-, -?-. Front row, third and eighth from left: Christine Evans, Gillian Cadman. *(Dorothy Ricketts)*

Lyng Junior Boys' School prefects, 1950. Back row, left to right: Alan Marshall, John Wyatt, Trevor Coles, Brian Richards, Keith Vincent. Front row: Patrick Smith, David Jones, Ray Corbett, Eddie Stone, Michael Woodfield. (*Eddie Stone*)

Lyng Junior School FC, 1972. Back row, left to right: Graham Cooper, -?-, Kiel Fieldhouse, Gilchrist Walters, Martin Jones, Kevin ?, -?-, -?-, Lee Dodd. Middle row: Andrew Henson, Alan Hughes, Martin Ralley, Gary Phillips, Andrew Rolf, Chris Minton, John Edwards. Front row: Craig Nicklin, Stephen Dye, Steven Edwards, Tony Giles, -?-, Roy Williams. (*Alan Hughes*)

Lyng Infants and Junior School, *c.* 1923. Fifth row, seventh and eighth from left: Alice Fletcher, Vera Knight. Fourth row, first and eighth: Eva Walsgrove, Gladys Herbert. Third row, ninth from left: Mary Gilbert. Second row, third: Irene Head. Front row: Mabel Sheldon, Janet Greaves, -?-, Elsie Robbins. (*Sheila Walsgrove*)

Spon Lane Secondary Modern Girls' School, 1951. Back row, left to right: Margaret White, June Long, Mavis Lawley, Linda Whitehouse, Pamela Cartwright. Middle row: Mavis Harris, Pamela Nicholas, Maureen Howes, Janet Yates, Maxine Martin, Jean Lloyd, Heather Davies, Jill Davies, Gillian Williams, Miriam Nock, Margaret Turford, June Walker. Front row: Valerie Howard, Gillian Healy, Thelma ?, Christine Howen, June Wilkes, Iris Jones, Valerie Povey, June Wallace, Pat Butwell, Sally Tyler, Brenda Ball, Sylvia Charlton. *(Janet Baker)*

Spon Lane Secondary Modern Boys School, Class 3A, 1948. Back row, left to right: Dickie Law, Don Picken, Alf Shutt, Ron Barnett, Alf Hickman, -?-, -?-, Ralph Nicholls, -?-, ? Corbett, ? Hopcroft. Middle row: ? Chisholm, David Keasey, -?-, -?-, -?-, -?-, Geoffrey Mayne, -?-, John Purshouse, -?-. Front row: ? Bates, -?-, Brian Chapman, Harold Beaumont, Ron France, -?-, Brian Snape, ? Greenaway, Brian Fletcher, Dennis Frampton, John Champion. *(Ron Barnett)*

Alderman Jack Williams, Mayor of West Bromwich, congratulates five gold winners of the Duke of Edinburgh's Award Scheme at Menzies High School, 19 January 1972. From left to right: Peter Tinsley, Pat Povey, Alan Slater, Alderman Jack Williams, Neil Woodyatt, Robert Shepherd. Other gold award winners were J. Hazeldeen, A. Garbett, B. Phillips, J. Walker, J. Spriggs, D. Dale, G. Saunders, R. Steventon, N. Whitehouse, R. Slater, D. Bowen. *(Jack Williams)*

Yew Tree Junior School's musical production of *The Wonderful Inn, c. 1972.* Back row, left to right: -?-, Ralph Graw, Claire Fullard, -?-, -?-, Martin Cannell, Timothy Wilkes. Middle row: Richard Coates, -?-, Nicholas Brown, Stephanie Ward, Leslie Hudson, Tracy Moran, Craig Bannister, -?-, Peter Garrett. Front row: Stephen Hall, Julie Bowater, Simon Wilkes, Andrea Lycett, Patricia Rolfe. *(Moreen Wilkes)*

Black Lake Primary School, *c.* 1956. Among the pupils at the back of the class, left: Linda Johnson, Mary Lloyd, Pat Jennings. Standing, centre: Olga Owen (teacher). Standing, extreme right: Mary Hubble. Second right: Pat ?. Fourth row from left to right: Derek? -?-, Linda Smith, -?-. Third row: Sandra Harris, -?-, Joyce Jeavons, -?-. Second row: Denise Shermer, Margaret Thompson, J. Hutchins, Deborah Turner. Front row: -?-, -?-, Jimmy Hibbs, Alan Talbot. *(Mary Loat)*

West Bromwich Town Schoolboys FC were the winners of the Leckie Shield after defeating Brierley Hill Schoolboys 2–1 in the final, season 1960/61. Back row, left to right: Jim Stevens, Roy Kirkpatrick, Trevor Bytheway, Phil Parkes, Robert Partridge, Alan Ledbury, Philip Speed, Keith Wright. Front row: Ken Sutera, Joe Foster, Colin Angel, Graham Turner, Paul Roberts. Phil Parkes eventually became a professional football player with Wolverhampton Wanderers and for many years was their first-team goalkeeper. *(Graham Turner)*

ACKNOWLEDGEMENTS

I would like to thank all of the many friends who have loaned me their precious photographs in order to make this second West Bromwich publication possible. In keeping with my previous books, all of the contributors' names have been acknowledged at the end of each caption.

My thanks are also extended to the following people for their help with additional information: Doris Abbotts, Annie Ball, John Bayliss, Ian Bott, Ted Brougham, Derek Chamberlain, Keith Cherrington, Ruth Cherrington, John Clark, Patrick Fahey, David Grigg, Graham Harper, Ivor Hodgetts, Keith Hodgkins, Margaret and Michael Holloway, Kathleen Homeshaw, Jim Houghton, Joan Howes, Deborah Leary, David Lord, David Malborn, Tony Matthews, Shirley Mauldridge, Andrew Maxam, Albert Murphy, Ciaran O'Carroll, Lily Phillips, Mary Powell, Alan Price, Mwyndeg Price, John Quance, Iris Reynolds, Michael Robinson, Ken Rock, Mary and Jim Rose, the Revd Fr John Sharp BA, Mth, PhD, Dorothy Smith, Betty and Ron Tedstone, Gladys Welsh, Sheila Whitehouse, Vera Whittaker, Jack Williams, Ned Williams, David Wilson, Graham Woodall, Ted Woodward.

I am also grateful to Asda (Great Bridge), BBC Radio WM, *Black Country Bugle*, *Black Country Mail*, Crown Cards, *Express & Star*, *Great Barr Observer*, Saga 105.7 FM, *Sandwell Chronicle*, Sandwell Community History and Archives Service, Sidney Darby & Son Ltd, *Walsall Observer*, Wesley Methodist Church and Circuit, West Bromwich Central Reference Library.

Thanks to everyone at Sutton Publishing, in particular: Helen Bradbury, Clive Burley, Paul Field, Simon Fletcher, Martin Latham, Michelle Tilling, Bow Watkinson, Jeremy Yates-Round.

Many thanks to Dr Carl Chinn MBE for his continued support and encouragement.

My special thanks once again to *Dawn Davey* for typing the manuscript.

Finally to my wife Beryl, for supporting me in everything I do.

Memories of 'Evergreen' Ivy Round-Hancock
1915–2005
Pictured with fellow concert party members, c. 1942.
Vida Round • Iris Howes • Dorothy Cooksey